S0-BWX-769

The Insecurity of Art

In memory of A.J.M. Smith,
first theoretician of Canadian modernism

The Insecurity of Art

Essays on Poetics

Edited by

Ken Norris & Peter Van Toorn

Published with the assistance of the Canada Council.
Cover artwork by Nancy Smith.
Cover graphics by JW Stewart.
Book design by Simon Dardick.

Robert Allen's "Post-Mortemism" has appeared in *Moosehead Review*.
Leonard Cohen's "How To Speak Poetry" has appeared in *Death of a Lady's Man*, McClelland and Stewart, the Canadian Publishers.
Louis Dudek's "What Ever Happened to Poetry" and "The Theory of the Image in Modern Poetry" have appeared in the Louis Dudek issue of *Open Letter*.
John Glassco's "A Real Good Noise" has appeared in the *Toronto Globe & Mail*.
Ralph Gustafson's "The Sequence" is extracted from *Sequences*, Black Moss Press.
Tom Konyves' "Videopoetry I" and "Poetika" have appeared in the *Montreal Journal of Poetics*.
Irving Layton's "Preface" is from *The Tightrope Dancer*, McClelland and Stewart, the Canadian publishers.
John McAuley's "Concrete Poetry: The Story of a Further Journey" has appeared in the *Montreal Journal of Poetics*.
Stephen Morrissey's "The Insecurity of Art" is from *The Trees of Unknowing*", Véhicule Press.
F.R. Scott's "Preface" is from *Poems of French Canada*, Blackfish Press.
David Solway's "The Flight From Canada" first appeared in *CVII*.
Richard Sommer's "A Deer On the Road and Practice" appeared in *CVII*.

Canadian Cataloguing in Publication Data
Main entry under title:
The Insecurity of art
ISBN 0-919890-42-3 (bound). - ISBN 0-919890-43-1 (pbk.)
1. Poetics—Addresses, essays, lectures. I. Norris, Ken, 1951- II. Van Toorn, Peter, 1944-
PN1064.I57 1982 808.1 C82-090131-8

Dépôt légal, Bibliothèque nationale du Québec and the National Library of Canada, 4th trimester, 1982.
Printed in Canada.

CONTENTS

INTRODUCTION

Like its social politics, the poetic politics of Quebec are far from complacent. There is little tendency on the part of Québécois poets, be they English or French, to opt for the status quo. One senses in artistic work from Quebec the impetus of controversy and transition. What unifies the essays in this volume is that they all seem to be calling for reassessment or breakthrough.

In this century English poetry in Quebec has embodied a curious synthesis of traditional knowledge and revolutionary fervour, at times aesthetically in harmony, but more often exemplified by factional warfare. We have only to look at the *Preview—First Statement* feud of the 1940's to see the roots of an aesthetic antagonism that has permeated Quebec poetry for the past forty years. With Quebec ever in the process of becoming, its English poets have fought the war of their own identity and that of their poetry, a war between the static and kinetic, the aristocratic and democratic, the cosmopolitan and native, between inherited and organic form, between poetical and social content. Out of the dynamism of this conflict has emerged a powerful, fully achieved poetry.

In many of these essays we hear a call for re-evaluation. Robert Allen asks us to put aside Post-Modernism, John Glassco to recognize the deceptive nature of poetry readings, Peter Van Toorn to throw off the mechanistic prosody that has been imposed upon twentieth century poetry by the use of the typewriter in composition, Stephen Morrissey to discard personal style, Anne McLean to put aside feminist concerns, David Solway to abandon the search for a Canadian content. These are harsh criticisms levelled at prevailing aesthetic trends. Beyond these criticisms, however, there are suggestions as to how the poet is to proceed. Leonard Cohen tells *how* to speak poetry if poetry is to be spoken, Louis Dudek insists on the primacy of "poem" over "process," D.G. Jones reaffirms Klein's calling for "a green inventory," Tom Konyves champions a new poetic medium, Irving Layton depicts the poet's dance on the tightrope strung between sex and death, love and loathing, Richard

Sommer announces an openness in art and experience, and Scott, Plourde and Jones show us how, through translation, we can, in some small measure, overcome the pain called Babel.

These essays emanate from a province where change and evolution are obviously at work in the lives of people every day. There is nothing about the social reality of life in Quebec that is mapped out with certainty. Life everywhere is always subject to change; it's just that here we are so much more aware of it. The foundation stone of the past is in place but it may not hold, and there may not be a good enough reason why it should. Looking to the future there are vast possibilities for social and political change; but change itself is not the end: desired change is.

To borrow and modify a Layton metaphor, the English poet in Quebec dances on a tightrope strung between past and future, tradition and innovation in both poetic and social senses. The present tense is that tightrope, and the dancing upon it is an experience that contains both apprehension and exhilaration. In his essay "The Insecurity of Art," Stephen Morrissey asserts that "the very joy & freedom of art & life is the hidden presence of insecurity." The English poet in Quebec writes his poetry, lives his life, and makes his aesthetic judgements under the personal and social conditions of that very insecurity.

Ken Norris
March 1, 1982

ROBERT ALLEN

Post-Mortemism

The term "dissociation of sensibility", coined by T.S. Eliot, has long been used as a paradigm for the kinds of alienation of which poets are victims—presumably in a way only quantitatively different from that of all human beings in a post-industrial era—as well as the fatal dichotomies of thought and feeling from which much of lyric poetry suffers. Eliot placed the crisis between Donne and Milton, but Eliot is notorious for his inability to see history in a dialectical way. Whatever his notion of the currents of thought between 1590 and 1660, he fails to find in Milton the "reaction of thought into feeling" characterizing Donne. Milton's earnest attempt to discourse about feeling presumably makes him incapable (so the argument runs) of real poetry. This sort of alienation is similar to Freudian alienation, in which subject and object are severed, and to Marxist alienation, in which workers are alienated both from the modes of production and from their own sense of productive activity. Eliot, however, confines his comments to the realm of aesthetics, a fatal blindness still characterizing much poetry and criticism. His aristocratic sense of history causes him to see Modernism as a product of the human imagination entirely, and not of the economic and social forces that generated the Modernists' world. Such a narrow view precludes him from seeing where the dissociation comes from. He can merely note that it is there.

Pound gives a similar account of the process, but using different personalities. He talks of the split between Cavalcanti—a contempory of Dante—and Petrarch, in whose hands the organic image became ornamental. This alienation is noted but not explained.

If modern poetry descends almost whole from Eliot and Pound, it is easy to see how the personalizing, unhistoric, formalist criticism of their era has fostered a poetry infected with romantic, hermeneutic visions; how the modern poet conceives himself to be a latterday *wandervogel*, alienated from his culture and his class. Pound and Eliot must have tried to rectify their own alienation, but had their thinking been dialectic they would have discovered that without changing human society they could not significantly have changed themselves.

At any rate, dissociation of sensibility was what the great modernist movements instinctively felt, and what they tried vainly, in movements as diverse as Dada, Expressionism, Vorticism, Imagism, etc., to overcome. Of the post-Romantic movements Symbolism was the first and most consequential. Its revolution lay in a theory of the suggestiveness of language generally and in the image or symbol in particular. It lay also in a distrust of "ordinary discourse". The world around them, infected with progress, industrialism, profit and so forth, became more and more the realm of naked statement. Language—plain language—described this tawdry world too well, and thus the language of art had to move towards obscuration. The theories of the symbolists offered nothing of a revolutionary nature, except perhaps the programmatic emphasis the theories themselves took. They are simply a new twist to the old form-content split, removed to an abstract level and buttressed by the terminology and assumptions of modern anthropology, depth psychology and linguistics. In linguistics, for example, we find the problem outlined in terms of denotation and connotation. In countless poetics, dating back to Aristotle, it is the tension between reason and intellect, imagination and passion. Edgar Allan Poe, whom the Symbolists idolized, makes an effort, in the introductory remarks to *Murders in the Rue Morgue*, to outline how the human psyche might become whole again, and to set the stage for his own creation, the detective Auguste Dupin, whose synthesis of the logical and the intuitive is supposed to represent that wholeness. Poe must have succeeded to some degree, for Dupin becomes the blueprint for 140 years of detective heroes and the Romantic synthesis in Poe's stories finally gives birth to Hollywood and the pulp thriller. The Symbolists, had they known it, were themselves perpetuating the dissociation of sensibility they feared, and in the process apotheosizing form at the expense of accurate observation. Perhaps more importantly they took the poet, already separated from the *hoi poloi* by romanticism, to a loftier position in human society: beyond moral responsibility; beyond the need to justify art in terms any more complex than poetic intent.

I have so far stressed the negative effects of Modernism—perhaps more obvious now because the movement dragged on so long: is still going strong, in fact. At the time, Symbolism and its offshoots were a natural corrective to the conventional language and feeling of a bourgeois poetry. Dada flourished for only three years before Tristan Tzara declared it dead; yet fifty years later, West Coast Dadaists continue to make guerilla warfare against something called "the Eastern poetry establishment", though they themselves are as plushly ensconced. Dada had to take art away from meaning into absurdity. In a New York exposition in the 1920's Marcel Duchamp exhibited a urinal. Nowadays a tantamount gesture would be to sneak into a display of urinal art with a Rembrandt. The point is that satire, derision, display—in short, the whole theory of anti-art—quickly run their effective course, and then must either dissipate and be replaced, or become codified into a new conventionality, which is what has happened in poetry today, where the academic vies with the avant-garde for Canada Council monies and a place in the academies. These two schools are two sides of the same coin: formalist, and in the end reactionary. To be a Surrealist, pure and simple, is as absurd an anachronism as to be a genteel lyricist, endlessly reflective and in the end without substance. Both modes are sentimental and bourgeois; both are noncritical, except in terms so meaningless as to disarm all criticism.

What is the avant-garde? There are two ways to answer this question. The first is that it is represented by those Canadian poets who term themselves avant-garde or post-modernist: bpNichol, bill bissett, George Bowering (and a host of others, predominantly West Coast, but also to be found in loosely-connected groups in Toronto and Montreal). The second is that there is no avant-garde in Canadian poetry: that it has been pre-empted by an increasingly conventionalized formalism and experimentalism which strives always to identify itself as progressive, in order to obscure the fact that it is bourgeois and reactive. (I have confined my remarks here to Canadian poetry, but much the same might be said, to a lesser or greater degree, of American, British, and presumably other post-modernist poetries.)

The Canadian avant-garde, as an ongoing, traditional mode—almost a fetishism—has its own rare moments of real Dada: one critic calls bpNichol the most revolutionary poet writing today. The Canada Council falls all over itself to support the new Dada imperialists. (Tzara said that if you drew attention to yourself by calling yourself Dada, you were not.) Poets from other lyric nurseries attempt to graft on Dada boughs, even those who until now have been true Canadian pines. The whole thing has descended to mannerism, and is as sterile as the worst academic poetry whose antithesis the avant-garde claims to be. It would have been better if Duncan, Olson, *et al*, had never visited British Columbia and left the fecund Black Mountain from which this mousy avant-garde springs; and sometimes I wish the Canada Council did not keep the whole enterprise of poetry going: we would all lose, but the good poets would lose less.

Certainly, state subsidy of the arts in Canada—at least as it relates to poetry—has increased the quality and cosmopolitanism of Canadian writing, but it has not yet eradicated a dangerous naïveté that makes readers accept almost any poetic claim, no matter how off the wall: *to accept intention as a validation of quality*. This is the natural evolution of a state-supported poetry that elevates the role of the poet above his social importance and invests him with the romantic aura of a world-fashioning minor deity. As a result, all of our criticism begs the question of meaning, preferring to deal in the flotsam and jetsam of post-modern formalism: images and symbols, no matter how nonreferential and banal; halfhearted association; gestures for the sake of gestures; erratic typography; sophomoric surrealism; fragments of sentences, trailing off into portentious silence; anti-art; anti-politics; obscurity and triviality purporting to represent a world full of obscurity and triviality...

As a result, the dissociation so feared by Pound and Eliot has come to pass in totality: hundreds of domesticated lyricists, obsequious in this court or that, permanently dissociated from their world and their class.

The battle for modernism was long since won. Most of the surrealism, symbolism and vorticism of the past seems tame, even ingenuous—as do many of the manifestos of post-symbolist movements. Pound's theories of the image and of musicality and emotion in poetry are second nature to every poet writing today. Pound also stressed craft and thought, and said that poets should not consider publishing just because they happen to scribble the odd bit of personal ephemera: this lesson unfortunately does not seem to have been learned so well.

I do not wish to discuss the avant-garde poets further. They disarm criticism and no doubt can dismiss what criticism they find here as intellectual cavilling, ignorant of their assumptions. Neither do I wish, however, to lionize the academic poetry that is the other side of bourgeois formalism. The discouraging thing is that the argument will not, in all likelihood, be taken up by either of the above groups, either because they must remain anti-critical in order to survive, or because they will assume I must be referring to someone else. If alienation is complete then the wide Styx between us, replete with murmurs of the dead and damned, will forever keep us apart, and the Canada Council, solicitous of both the dead and the quick, will keep us all going with the ready cash, and let us all flourish equally.

I have not here proposed my own poetic, nor that of the *Moosehead Review*. Suffice it to say that no art can be worthwhile that does not, to paraphrase Marx, awaken the world from its own dream and explain to the world its own acts. The Surrealists originally shouted, after Goethe, "One must dream! One must act!" Somewhere along the line the revolutionary fervour went out of this sentiment and dreaming and acting became once more the polar chambers of a passionless heart. The cynicism of much modern avant-garde may have already been present when Breton, Bunuel and Aragon gave up in despair and joined the Communist party, leaving the rest of the surrealists behind in the randomness of pure art. That much of poetry has continued to be "the dream" and ceased being "the act" is incontestable. In the work of poets whose world-view is undissociated, the lyric elements are not easily separated from the socio-dramatic matrix of the poem—another way of saying that the irony is structural rather than formal. Eliot saw this quality in Dante, Shakespeare and Donne, for whom thought and feeling were inseparable—for whom, in fact, the rhetorical polarity could not even be conceived of. The post-modern (or as someone has phrased it, post-mortem) lyric can bridge the gulf neither by form nor non-form (since both, at the bottom, are formal approaches). The way out of this bind is not form-tinkering. Neither is it going "beyond language" into the murk of process—a kind of mysticism of which the avant-garde is decidedly fond. Experiment with form is not likely to produce a substantial new poetic, at least not in itself. Reworking Huron or Haida legends into fragmentary poetic narratives is not progressive. It is a reactionary scam. The writing of history without historical analysis is specious; it can lead only to sentimentalism, a mode now in favour, judging from the banal retelling of prairie childhoods, the empty evocation of depression days and schoolbook history, the recapitulation of borrowed or stolen myths, and so forth, characterizing much of the poetry of the 1970's. This is not our world. It can be made ours—or part of ours—with some effort and intelligence. Without penetration by political and cultural awareness, however, literature is just "literary", as the Dada and Surrealist movement knew from the beginning; as Mayakovski knew, and Lorca; as Berryman and Neruda knew; and the older Yeats, forsaking the Celtic Twilight. Eliot and Pound did not know, or did not show they knew. Consequently most of their followers in Britain and the United States retreated into their private, confessionalist selves. The most expansive and inclusive escape it: Lowell, Wright, Larkin, Ashbery; but the fragmentary and alienated still remains the basic mode. Even among those I have just named there are problematic elements. Milton Acorn (one of the few poets in Canada to be fully aware of the problem, and to write in the light of that awareness) owes much to Lowell—specifically his development of the Jackpine Sonnet—but cannot adequately explain or condone Lowell's obscurity.

Too much of our poetry, therefore, is "literary"; this goes for the so-called avant-garde as much as for the academic lyricists; the transformation of the academic confessionalist lyric, with its limited powers of analysis and its dependence on irony, into the paralinguistic icon of the West Coast should not be—and in fact is not—our avant-garde.

No intelligent examination of the world in which we all live and must try to understand can possibly result in either formal ironies or formlessness and non-sense. Both modes deny implicitly that the world can be changed. They fall, morally, into the cynical gulf that Eliot himself enlarged. Both are complicated in the worst sense: they mystify; they are, equally, sophisticated shrugs. Real complexity—the sort generated by engagement with the world—can manifest itself in language as dense, images as powerful, and forms as demanding as the most extravagantly conceived "avant-garde" or the most finickally wrought academic formalism. Since the Surrealists, however, and possibly since the Symbolists, a certain kind of willful obscurity has been a part of poetry, enabling the merely clever poet to masquerade as the complex one. Bad poets assume a mode enabling them to construct a simulacrum that cannot, at first glance, be told from the genuine article; and our deep desire to pursue our own dreams and acts, while others pursue theirs, causes us not to want to be too critical of one another—to live and let live. The result is a confirmation and extension of our dissociation, and of a thousand private worlds that penetrate one another only on the most trivial levels. The easy solution is to say goodbye to the "splendid trifles" of lyric poetry for art forms that appear to be of more moment, just as the Surrealists deserted the lyric for the polemic and the satire. We must find forms that have the world to talk about—but the world has never been without poetry; it is up to writers not to desert life: neither to forsake dialectic for easy paradox nor the world for its shadow.

Tristan Tzara declared Dada dead. Who will do the same for Post-Modernism?

STEPHEN BROCKWELL

Empathy in Modern Verse

It is obvious that art should have an impact on both the intellectual and sensual functions of the observer. To truly unify these functions in a single aesthetic experience requires an aesthetic sense not always found in Western art. The term *einfühlung* has been used to describe this empathetic relation, which is more simply phrased as "feel-in". This implies that the observer not only examines the art work, but feels a unity with the work, in effect becomes transfixed in time for a moment, his senses and intellect liberated by the experience of appreciation.

The poetry of the English language has been often criticised for a dryness which I will try to demonstrate with two lines by Keats. Often quoted, well loved by some, they are, in the essence of this essay, a little in-empathetic:

> Beauty is truth, truth beauty,—that is all
> Ye know on earth, and all ye need to know.

These lines are closer to criticism (admittedly an art in itself) than poetry as an empathetic release of the senses and intellect. His statement about art may be valid, but should such a statement about art be made so blatantly *in* the art? It should not be up to the poet to tell the reader what he is saying. The poet must let the ideas unfold on their own in the reader's mind at the reader's pace. Let the poem be a bit of mystery and, although the poem may not be entirely understood, which is regrettable, the important thing is to release the senses with an evocative image so that the mind may unconsciously or consciously feel the thought. This is true especially in modern times, when the mind and body are subject to so many states of over and under stimulation. It often takes years for a poem to be understood: if the poet releases the reader for a few moments from this world so that the meaning of the poem is pursued, then he has accomplished as much as can be asked of the art. Take for example the seventeenth century Japanese poet Basho:

ah! the ancient pond
a frog leaps in—
no sound but the water's sigh.

(Translation mine.) The translation rarely does justice to the original but the essence of empathy *is* expressed in the poem. There is an image of broken stillness—the sound, the sight, and perhaps even the touch and taste of stillness are inflected in the poem. The senses are released, and if the poem is read as was intended (over and over until the words mesh with the fibre of the mind) the understanding of not only broken stillness, but of the impermanence of life as well comes through. To compare another line by Keats:

The poetry of earth is never dead.

What seems to be missing here is the *sense* that the poetry of earth never dies. What use can there be in beginning a poem with a single line that explains, quite simply, exactly what the rest of the poem will be about? None. This is an in-empathetic line. Not only Keats but Wordsworth, Donne, Byron and many English poets, great poets of our language, are missing the aesthetic sense that the image has brought into modern verse.

Pound's "In a Station of the Metro" is a superb Imagist poem:

The apparition of these faces in the crowd;
Petals on a wet black bough.

In this single couplet more is said about beauty, about impermanence, about the fruitlessness of modern life (in 1912) than could have been said in many good English poems before Imagism.

One quality in the poetry of Wallace Stevens is its blending of both image and philosophy so that the poem is an empathetic philosophical contemplation. In his later poetry, however, Stevens became so philosophical that the poems are less image and more pure thought; a reader not well acquainted with philosophy would not find his poems rewarding because they offer little other than abstract words of thought (Wallace Stevens saw no difficulty in this). A poem should not be so restricting and unattainable. The great poems of the language can be understood on different levels by all; they give pleasure to those who understand little else and wisdom to those who look for it. Frost for example:

One can do worse than be a swinger of birches.

Although this is not an Imagist line it is still an evocative, empathetic line—suggesting thought in the natural language of a deceptively simple phrase.

It can't be said that a poem should contain no thought—that is ridiculous—what a poem should do is have the thought so expressed that it is not so obvious that the reader is left dissatisfied both sensually and intellectually. Let the thought develop through image, sound, and language. There is no need to tell the reader what the poem is saying; let the reader find out in his own time. This could be considered one of the problems with much of the bad poetry in Canada these days. Poets seem to be too often ignoring the image and even the music of poetry to get a completely personal statement that is often interesting to no one but the poet. This personalism cannot go far for the reader, a personality is too easily expressed today in abstract terms. James Tate seems to be on the right track when he says

> Beware the Warden of Light has married
> an old piece of string.

LEONARD COHEN

How to Speak Poetry

Take the word butterfly. To use this word it is not necessary to make the voice weigh less than an ounce or equip it with small dusty wings. It is not necessary to invent a sunny day or a field of daffodils. It is not necessary to be in love, or to be in love with butterflies. The word butterfly is not a real butterfly. There is the word and there is the butterfly. If you confuse these two items people have the right to laugh at you. Do not make so much of the word. Are you trying to suggest that you love butterflies more perfectly than anyone else, or really understand their nature? The word butterfly is merely data. It is not an opportunity for you to hover, soar, befriend flowers, symbolize beauty and frailty, or in any way impersonate a butterfly. Do not act out words. Never act out words. Never try to leave the floor when you talk about flying. Never close your eyes and jerk your head to one side when you talk about death. Do not fix your burning eyes on me when you speak about love. If you want to impress me when you speak about love put your hand in your pocket or under your dress and play with yourself. If ambition and the hunger for applause have driven you to speak about love you should learn how to do it without disgracing yourself or the material.

What is the expression which the age demands? The age demands no expression whatever. We have seen photographs of bereaved Asian mothers. We are not interested in the agony of your fumbled organs. There is nothing you can show on your face that can match the horror of this time. Do not even try. You will only hold yourself up to the scorn of those who have felt things deeply. We have seen newsreels of humans in the extremities of pain and dislocation. Everyone knows you are eating well and are even being paid to stand up there. You are playing to people who have experienced a catastrophe. This should make you very quiet. Speak the words, convey the data, step aside. Everyone knows you are in pain. You cannot tell the audience everything you know about love in every line of love you speak. Step aside and they will know what you know because they know it already. You have nothing to teach them. You are not more beautiful than they are. You are not wiser. Do not shout at them. Do not force a dry entry. That is bad sex. If you show the lines of your genitals, then deliver what you promise. And remember that people do not really want an acrobat in bed. What is our need? To be close to the natural man, to be close to the natural woman. Do not pretend that you are a beloved singer with a vast loyal audience which has followed the ups and downs of your life to this very moment. The bombs, flame-throwers, and all the shit have destroyed more than just the trees and villages. They have also destroyed the stage. Did you think that your profession would escape the general destruction? There is no more stage. There are no more footlights. You are among the people. Then be modest. Speak the words, convey the data, step aside. Be by yourself. Be in your own room. Do not put yourself on.

This is an interior landscape. It is inside. It is private. Respect the privacy of the material. These pieces were written in silence. The courage of the play is to speak them. The discipline of the play is not to violate them. Let the audience feel your love of privacy even though there is no privacy. Be good whores. The poem is not a slogan. It cannot advertise you. It cannot promote your reputation for sensitivity. You are not a stud. You are not a killer lady. All this junk about the gangsters of love. You are students of discipline. Do not act out the words. The words die when you act them out, they wither, and we are left with nothing but your ambition.

Speak the words with the exact precision with which you would check out a laundry list. Do not become emotional about the lace blouse. Do not get a hard-on when you say panties. Do not get all shivery just because of the towel. The sheets should not provoke a dreamy expression about the eyes. There is no need to weep into the handkerchief. The socks are not there to remind you of strange and distant voyages. It is just your laundry. It is just your clothes. Don't peep through them. Just wear them.

The poem is nothing but information. It is the Constitution of the inner country. If you declaim it and blow it up with noble intentions then you are no better than the politicians whom you despise. You are just someone waving a flag and making the cheapest appeal to a kind of emotional patriotism. Think of the words as science, not as art. They are a report. You are speaking before a meeting of the Explorers' Club or the National Geographic Society. These people know all the risks of mountain climbing. They honour you by taking this for granted. If you rub their faces in it that is an insult to their hospitality. Tell them about the height of the mountain, the equipment you used, be specific about the surfaces and the time it took to scale it. Do not work the audience for gasps and sighs. If you are worthy of gasps and sighs it will not be from your appreciation of the event, but from theirs. It will be in the statistics and not the trembling of the voice or the cutting of the air with your hands. It will be in the data and the quiet organization of your presence.

Avoid the flourish. Do not be afraid to be weak. Do not be ashamed to be tired. You look good when you're tired. You look like you could go on forever. Now come into my arms. You are the image of my beauty.

How to Speak Poetry

I did not want to appear again in these pages except to say goodbye. I thought that he should be left alone in this most delicate phase of the wedding preparation, with the man asleep and the woman being born. I thought he could be trusted to maintain the balance. He can't. It is too quiet for him. He has to shoot off his fucking Sunday School mouth. We're supposed to sit back and listen to The Good Guy talking, the old crapulous Dogma of Decency. This filth cannot go unpunished. How dare he summon the widows of Asia to his side! How dare he break his vow of silence to lecture, in the name of The People, from the shit-stained marble balcony of his obscene cultural delusions! I hate him for this. He will pay for this religious advertisement. He will carry the syrup of it in his balls. He will pass this life as a teddy bear. Death to the Commissars of the Left and the Right! Death to the Commissars of Mystery! I hate his fucking face, all serious with concern. Don't let him into the good movie, and don't let him hear any of the merry tunes in the Music Hall. Never let him sing again. And let him sit outside with his stinking educational corpse while the stripper on the little gilded stage turns every one of us on.

LOUIS DUDEK

Whatever Happened to Poetry?

I wonder whether you have noticed, as I have, for some time now, that poetry has virtually disappeared from our society.

It doesn't matter as it used to. Even in the universities it has been pushed aside, from first place to fifth or sixth; no longer 'required' in the humanities; neglected by the English departments. In the high schools, say the teachers, it is 'the hardest subject to teach.' Nobody wants it.

Poetry has vanished from the editorial page, in the newspapers, where it once had a firm foothold. (In television it never got a toe-hold.) Formerly quoted in the House of Commons as a matter of course, by such people as Disraeli and Gladstone, it is hardly ever quoted now—some say because there is nothing worth quoting—either here or in England. If it is quoted, it is misquoted or misapplied. I find an example or two in the Canadian Hansard:

> *A Kingdom for a Horse* has been somewhat changed. Now it is a horse for a queen... Is there any foundation for the suggestion made in Western Canada that the RCMP Farm, which produces the horses that have been used by the RCMP, is to be closed down? (John Diefenbaker, May, 1969)

In another example a parliamentarian applies Hamlet to economics: 'Naturally, we all want government departments to balance their budgets. That is a consummation devoutly to be wished...'

Of course, in modern times, poetry has never been a popular art. You'd have to go back to the days of Homer for that, or the primitive culture of the Anglo-Saxons in England (called the Dark Ages). They had no television, no topless night clubs, and no girlie magazines in those dark days, so they actually turned to poetry for entertainment.

But even if poetry hasn't been popular, with us, it has counted with a considerable minority at times. One of Byron's books sold 14,000 copies in a single day; his publisher Murray said that the poet had earned the equivalent of $375,000 within a ten-year period.

Alexander Pope bought himself a house at Twickenham with the proceeds from a translation of Homer's Iliad. One reads that 'the great Victorian poets'—Longfellow, Tennyson, Browning—'commanded a huge public in their own day; people waited for the publication of their new volumes with the eagerness of a line waiting to buy tickets for a popular play.'

But money, or popularity, isn't really the point. It is the great prestige in which poetry was held, the almost-reverence for the highest of the arts, that we have lost and that we are now regretting. It's as if religion fell into decline first and poetry dropped off afterward. Robert Hillyer writes of 'the blank indifference to poetry of the modern public.' Karl Shapiro has a book called *The Poetry Wreck*. In all public places there is a dead silence about poetry, it has vanished from our society. As the Montreal poet A.M. Klein once wrote, '...from our real society he has disappeared...' (i.e. the poet) 'he simply does not exist.'

The reason, some might want to say—as Hillyer and Shapiro do say—must lie partly with the poets. Yes, certainly. The artists have departed from our society; they have turned their backs on the public. This is one thing we must understand. All the arts in our time have turned away from the public.

Consider, in this light, the great revolution in art that we call Modernism. In each of the arts you will find the artists turning away from and rejecting precisely the element in their art that the public considered essential—the very thing that people desired and praised in that art. In painting it was the lively depiction of a subject, the resemblance to some recognizable aspect of reality in the world. The modern painters, turning to abstraction, disappointed the expectations of their public. In music it was melody, harmony and lively rhythm—in fact, tonality, that makes the first two possible—that were abandoned by the moderns. If you look into Otto Deri's history of modern music, *Exploring Twentieth-Century Music*, you will find that the modern system early abandoned even the assumption that music should please the ear, or arouse desirable emotions in the hearer. It rejected this expectation of the public, just as painting rejected verisimilitude of depiction. And in poetry, which is our subject, modernism abandoned rhyme and meter, that feature which for the average person coming out of the nineteenth century was pretty much the definition of poetry.

More than that, poetry abandoned the idea of easy comprehensibility—the basis of communication with a large audience—so it automatically excluded the public. Indeed, all the arts simply rejected the criterion of beauty, as it was traditionally accepted, as the objective of art; and so they disappointed the expectations of the public.

So there it is, if you want to blame the artists. But the artists do not turn their face away from their society unless the society is somehow disappointing them. They turn away if it is too ugly to look at. If it is ignorant and indifferent. Or if it is falsely seductive and dangerous to them. Ours is a very large democratic society, the mass society that results from improved medicine, universal education, and modern industrial production. It is hungry for goods and entertainments. The lust for entertainment, of course, is nothing new. All corrupt societies have known it. In past times, kings and their courts demanded luxuries and diversions in great quantity. They had huge banquets, tournaments, hunting, dancing, music and masques—and a thousand wives—to keep them entertained. Today the great democratic public is king; and its luxuries and entertainments are spread out in supermarkets and department stores, they run riot with 'violence and sex' on TV and in films, and they command the field of culture, as popular literature.

When this system of industrial expansion and cultural democracy was in its beginning, in the last century, the artists sometimes were able to see it as a great promising opportunity. The idea of perfectibility, taken from the French Enlightenment, was carried over into the nineteenth century of universal literacy and universal suffrage. Poets such as Longfellow and Tennyson rode on the tide, and cheapened their sensibility, one might say, by adjusting to the taste of the public. But this was only a first stage, a honeymoon stage, of the relation of the artist to society. Popular poetry became horribly mawkish, it became mindless and indulgent. The emotional plague characteristic of the middle class—and we are all of the middle class by now—is sentimentality; it surfaces whenever entertainment reaches the great audience—in 'The Sound of Music,' in soap opera, in 'All in the Family'—in books like *Jonathan Livingstone Seagull* and *Love Story*. And, of course, being brainless, sentimentality splits up into the reality it conceals, 'sex and violence,' whenever the truth breaks through: for sentimentality-sickness can be a cover-up for the primitive urges in their ugliest form. And so sentimentality is the way that poetry took before the beginning of modernism: it covered up Victorian sex and violence. (For the reality, in Victorian England, you look into such books as *My Secret Life* and *The Other Victorians*; or Charles Booth's *Life and Labour of the People in London* or Seebohm Rowntree's *Poverty*.)

Let me quote you a poem of the late-nineteenth century from a scholarly anthology. Anthologies are expected to present only the best of a period, so you can't fault me for picking out a rotten poem deliberately. Here, then, is one of the choice poems of the Nineties:

> It was a bowl of roses:
> There in the light they lay,
> Languishing, glorying, glowing
> Their life away.
>
> And the soul of them rose like a presence,
> Into me crept and grew,
> And filled me with something—someone—
> O, was it you?

The poem is perfectly suitable for a Valentine card.

No objection, if this were just a silly sentimental poem. But we know it is highly representative—it is actually by William Ernest Henley. It's representative of the kind of thing, at the popular level, that most readers at the turn of the century considered to be poetry. (They still do, and put it on their birthday greeting cards and Christmas cards: or perhaps they don't—perhaps poetry has vanished from our society even more completely than I thought, and it no longer occurs even in Hallmark greeting cards. I don't know. It did until very recently.)

[Incidentally, stationery stores do a thriving business in North America. They usually sell a few books as a sideline. Greeting cards are the *billets doux* of an illiterate society which has substituted printed clichés for personal messages.]

We are speaking about a mindless society. There was an interesting example of this in *Scribner's* magazine at the turn of the century. A lady sent in some of her husband's poetry for publication, with the following note:

> Dear Sir,
> My husband has always been a successful blacksmith. Now he is old and his mind is slowly weakening so he has taken to writing poems, several of which I enclose herewith.

Humour is always revealing, as Dr. Martin Grotjahn tells us in his book *Beyond Laughter*. All you have to do is take the bit of humour seriously and you will see what the subconscious is hiding from your attention—but wants to bring out for a friendly airing. Of course we 'don't mean it'! But then, at the same time, that's what we really do mean: in this case, that poetry is for those 'whose mind is slowly weakening.' It's what poetry had come to.

And therefore Modernism. Modernism, in short, was a turning away from the middle-class public, a turning away from inane and sentimental poetry. Hence its ironic dryness, its wasteland bitterness, and its extreme difficulty. But this is only the beginning of the story. There is the whole history of the avant-garde, and the reaction to the avant-garde, to be told—very briefly—to get us to where we are.

At the very highest intensity, where important things happen, modern art became experimental, and in turning away from the audience it turned in upon itself, upon the medium of art. In doing this it became an art for the few, not for the many. 'I join these words for four people,' as Ezra Pound said, '—some others may overhear them.'

As we know, this modern poetry demanded a great deal from its readers. It also demanded a new breed of critics. T.S. Eliot, said Robert Graves, 'asked the reader to find, despite the continual change of subject and meter, a connecting thread of sense.' *The Waste Land* has been called Cubism in poetry, and it required critics who knew almost everything and who had to make a very close study of the text to come up to this poetry. 'The entire school of so-called 'New Criticism," it has been said, 'came into being not only under Eliot's influence but as an instrument for the analysis of his work.'

A further consequence of this difficult poetry was that a generation arose, of both critics and students—mainly university people—between 1930 and 1950, who aspired to be equal to this kind of poetry and criticism. They were called, as some of us will remember, 'intellectuals.' The current use of the word 'elite', as a disparaging term, indicates a rejection; 'intellectual' was a term of approval, 'elite' is not. But T.S. Eliot was an elitist, Ezra Pound was an elitist, James Joyce was an elitist, W.B. Yeats was an elitist. In other words, we have a reaction against this modern tradition in the present rage for simple and popular forms of art.

Though there were very few genuine intellectuals, and very few really good critics in that line, the general type proliferated. They captured the universities, in their quiet way, and they became the 'establishment' of literature, by the 1950's. So much for the one phase of Modernism.

Very soon after, the Jacobins arrived on the scene and a new revolution occurred. After all, the intellectual position does not go well with the great majority—it gives them the mental cramps, and an inferiority complex. Especially as the universities and high schools expanded after the war, an immense pressure of resentment was built up, perhaps against education itself (since education is an elitist enterprise), but certainly against the difficult textual demands of poetry and literature among other subjects. The result was a massive teen-age revolt, the Beat and Hippie movement, whose aftermath we are now passing through.

Ginsberg's *Howl* (1957) and Beat poetry in general were the spearhead of a literary movement, and as such they were a powerful reaction against the Eliot-Auden line. But the movement of the Beats and the Hippies was more than mere literature. It was part of a massive barbarization of society that has ravaged our world for two decades now—though it has abated at the moment—and that affects everything, from the newspapers we read to the howling noise that fills the popular wave band on the radio.

There is no need to belabor the barbarism of Rock music or the return to savagery of the youth movement of the 1960's. Sufficient to remark that it has affected every department of life—including education and religion—but especially the whole field of entertainment and the arts.

[I might remark, just to complicate things, that barbarism is not the worst that can happen in human affairs. It's messy, but it has its points. Barbarism at least has energy, and it is not exclusive. Basically, it refuses to discriminate. In the end, it assimilates and renews what it conquers. Much worse than barbarism, really, is an exhausted and rigid refinement. Barbarism is primitive vitality. There is the early modern Greek poem by C.P. Cavafy, 'Waiting for the Barbarians', in which the officials of a town return sadly after their tense preparations to meet the barbarians, with the statement 'there are no barbarians any longer.' For, the poem concludes, 'Those people were a kind of solution.' In actual reality, however, the barbarians are always with us; a modern critic has written about 'The Barbarian Within'—an inexhaustible source—but there are plenty also outside the walls. I am not interested, however, in encouraging the barbarian; we have too much of him already. I am interested in civilization, made, if you like, out of nothing, but aiming for 'the peak of Popocatepetl.']

In any case, Allen Ginsberg and his friends represent in poetry this phase of barbarization which has swept over western society. You remember how the poem 'Howl' begins:

> I saw the best minds of my generation destroyed by madness, starving hysterical naked
> dragging themselves through the negro streets at dawn looking for an angry fix,
> angelheaded hipsters burning for the ancient heavenly connection to the starry dynamo in the machinery of night,
> who poverty and tatters and hollow-eyed and high sat up smoking in the supernatural darkness of cold-water flats floating across the tops of cities contemplating jazz...

In Canada there are now hordes of poets who follow this line of simplification and regression as the accepted way of poetry. Groups like the Four Horsemen, who perform on the stage with hammers, tin pans and other noise-makers; or poets who produce 'Smudge Concrete'—messy sheets of typewriter skids—sometimes completely illegible; or poets who wail into the microphone without pronouncing any recognizable words—are fair examples of the general trend. Better known, less extreme, are poets like Al Purdy, Joe Rosenblatt, George Bowering, who seem to write abundantly in the general stream of simplified poetry since the 1960's. In Montreal, currently, we have a monumental book entitled *Montreal English Poetry of the Seventies*[1] that belongs, for the most part, to this movement.

This is actually a rather interesting book. It contains all kinds of things—even some good poems. This is Stephen Morrissey's poem scored for 67 voices reading the one line of poetry:

> regard as sacred the disorder of my mind.

There is Ken Norris' little poem called 'Green Onions':

> I slept last night
>   with green onions
> Under my pillow
>   and I dreamed
> Strange dreams.

There is Bob McGee's memorable refrain:

> in the metro people come & go
> talking of mayor jean drapeau.

There is Marquita Crevier on modern love:

> It was not until I had lain in seven
> different beds to forget you
> that I remembered I had never loved you
> and it was not until I had searched
> my entire desk for your letter
> that I remembered there was no letter.

There are excellent poems: Peter Van Toorn's 'The Cattle', Anne McLean's 'Fête de St-Jean Baptiste', John McAuley's 'I Am Sending You A Valentine' and 'The Heart of the Matter', Stephen Morrissey's poem beginning—

> I am aiming for the hermetic statement
> for the totally inaccessible wotnot
>
> for stardust & gibberish
> & a wind that blows up suddenly

& rubs its back against the side of the house
creating new music and new seasons

spring is a butterfly that passes
before our eyes & then is gone

a sound that is shaped like a mouth
& then two sounds which hold lengthy conversations

& finally a blizzard in which there is only one sound
which is a finger rubbing against a pane of glass...

And Marc Plourde's 'In Park Extension'; and Dave Solway's poems, 'New England Poets', 'In Defence of Marriage'; and a number of other poems that are well worth ploughing for.

But the wild extravagance of the book is symptomatic. It's *a sensation*, it's *fan-tastic*. Like Rock-&-Roll the new poetry has a large following, mainly among young people under twenty-five. But this audience is not reliable; certainly it is not permanent. It comes and goes, it is soon replaced by another generation of teens. It's an audience that can vanish quickly. 'We're all famous for 15 minutes,' said what's-his-name, the Dada artist who was very famous a few years ago—Andy Warhol. Therefore the success, for the moment, of certain kinds of reductive and barbarized poetry does not mean that poetry is alive and well. The youth culture, with its enthusiasms and crazes, cannot sustain an art form, any more than the youth movement of the Sixties could reform the universities or renew education. It cannot develop a positive taste, or lead to a real new creative direction in art. (In any case, such a result is never achieved by gangs of people, but only by solitary individuals; and that is what we do not have—we have merely gangs and mob movements.)

So the popularity of a certain kind of poetry—the huge 'poetry readings', the multitude of subsidized books, the singing and performing poets celebrated in weekend newspapers—is no sign that we are living in an age of great poetry, or that poetry is thriving in our culture. Rather, it is a sign that poetry, like almost everything else in this bread-and-circus culture, has gone rotten. (Rock-&-Roll is no evidence that we're passing through a great age of music; after a hundred and years or so, if anybody is interested, it may be evidence that even popular music deteriorated in this century to loud repetitive roaring.) In fact, the present popularity of various kinds of degraded poetry is only proof of the collapse of poetry as an art form in our time.

Now we seem to have hit rock bottom. But I do not want to leave such an account without some positive attention to the future. And to find this, I must go a bit back, to the point where I said the modern arts turned in upon themselves and began to examine their own medium.

This happened because in the nineteenth century art had become very important—the very opposite of the unimportance it has now. It's an odd story. During the nineteenth century, following the Romantic re-routing, poetry became virtually a kind of religion, or a substitute for religion, replacing the personal God of Christianity. Nature was the altar of this new faith. And as the century wore on, and the inessentials seemed to be stripped away, art—or poetry—emerged as the supreme holy-of-holies, the door to the ineffable.

This, of course, is a familiar story. But not all of it. Since art, or art-for-art's-sake, was clearly of such supreme importance, and since we live in a highly analytic age, it became the artist's main preoccupation—even obsession—to examine the nature of art itself, through art. (As Ad Reinhardt says in his absolute way: 'Art-as-Art is a concentration on Art's essential nature...' and 'An avant-garde in Art advances Art-as-Art or it isn't an avant-garde.') It's as if the lover had become so enamored of his beloved's beauty that he took to the microscope and the tools of anatomy to discover the source of that mystery.

We know how the painters became interested in the nature of paint, in the nature of color itself, and in the nature of pure forms, to explore the possiblities of their medium. We know how the musicians began to explore the nature of sound, and eventually abandoned their instruments, for concrete noises and experiments with electronic sound. We know how poets became fascinated with the separate image, deprived of meter and rhyme, and how they ended with the projection of 'a heap of broken images' (a phrase from T.S. Eliot's *Waste Land*) or the epic accumulation of disconnected 'ideograms', fragments of history and macaronic poetry (in the *Cantos* of Ezra Pound), to write a poetry which few people could understand.

The reason for this is that the poets, too, became interested in the nature of poetry in the new sense, as a pure thing for itself, and this led them into arcane experiments of a higher poetic, leaving the general reader behind. If we keep in touch with the experimental avant-garde, which is the essential line of progression in any art, we find that these experiments eventually led to 'found poetry'—where the poet simply arranged the words of some bit of prose readily, transforming it into poetry; it led to 'concrete poetry,' in which a single word or even a single letter was typographically explored on the page; and it led to such things as improvised poetry, automatic poetry, and non-verbal sound recitation—each of these probing into the secret sources of the creative process.

In this progression in the experimental arts—whether in painting, in music, or in poetry—it is the inevitable paradox that 'art as art' has destroyed itself. 'Art for Art' leads to 'Art against Art.' 'Warhol correctly foresaw the end of painting,' says critic Gregory Battcock, 'and became its executioner.' '...Resulting solutions threaten the existence of sculpture as it has traditionally been conceived,' says Jack Burnham in *Beyond Modern Sculpture*. Modern music, writes Otto Deri, culminates in 'harshness of sound...distortion, dissolution and pulverization of its elements.' The latest developments, John Cage & Co., he notes, 'Do not qualify as music.'

What are we to say of poetry? I think I have said enough. In the current issue of the *Atlantic* (Oct. 1977), Donald Hall, a reputable critic, finds great merit in the following poem:

> The bird
> flies
> out the
> window. She
> flies.

This is still poetry that one can quote—and that from the *Collected Poetry* of one of the most highly regarded American poets, Robert Creeley. (Of course I have loaded the dice.) Take a rather interesting example from a Canadian avant-garde poet, bpNichol:

> roam
> ro m
> room
>
> rororo
> ao
> mmm
>
> ram
> om om
> ro ro
>
> ror
> am mo
> o mr o

Obviously there is poetry that one cannot read aloud, that onc can only look at. And there is poetry that one cannot even look at, poetry that one doesn't *want* to look at.

Is it any wonder, then, that John Fowles, author of *The Magus* and *The French Lieutenant's Woman*, remarks *en passant* in a current interview?—

I think we've had quite enough of avant-garde art in the 20th century...

This is very sad. We see two cul-de-sacs butting each other for a hopeful exit. Thus, there is one kind of development in experimental poetry—from French Symbolist to Concrete Poetry—which should be called *mainline modernism*. It is usually very intelligent, in its theory, very obscure or hermetic, and very demanding. Poets like Louis Zukofsky, an Objectivist, or Phyllis Webb in Canada, who is a kind of minimalist—writing very brief poems—or Victor Coleman in Toronto, who writes 'fragmentary, ikonic...private' poetry, and 'estimates that a good reader might understand 10% of most of his books, but that if he wrote to give more comprehension, the accuracy of the work would be impaired...'—these are mainline modernists.

Here is an example from the poetry of Victor Coleman:

> What is labor is a man works for some walking
> as he talks & the air spells some words of a language
> there is no eas-
> y access to
> E - (empty)[2]

But quite distinct and often antithetical to these are the poets I call barbarizers, who might also be called *populist*, opposed to high culture. Frank Davey says they celebrate 'a dark, chaotic but life-giving universe.' Among them is Michael Ondaatje, author of *Rat Jelly*, a poet of blood and violence. His Billy the Kid is a hero who 'reshapes his world with anger and bullets'—like the terrorists we read about in the newspapers. Another representative is Bill Bissett, about whom we read that 'his contempt for orthodox society has caused him to be ejected from cross-Canada trains, evicted by countless landlords, beaten, harrassed by police, and arrested and sentenced to prison.' His 'contempt for the orthodoxies of the printed word' have caused him to be regarded as 'a wild man or a freak.' At the same time he is said to be a poet of 'pure joy, energy, and spontaneous form.'[2]

So we see that in the current activity the two branches of poetry, esotericism or mainline modernism and the barbarism I have discussed earlier, come together in a doubtful union. The late products of a very proud, very intense aesthetic movement of poetry collides in confusion with the drippings and dribblings of the new barbarism which arose in the 1950's as a reaction to intellectual modernism. And to both kinds of poetry the bulk of society is utterly indifferent. It really cares neither for the avant-garde nor for the barbaric counter-avant-garde. This is the situation of poetry.

★

However, 'the end is not the end.' There is always a new beginning.

Let me ask, if you were writing poetry, what would you do? You can write anything you like, of course: the whole idea of imagination is freedom, to explore the possibilities of existence. But suppose you were lucky enough to write significant poetry, poetry that advances the art, opens up new worlds of poetry? What would it be?

We can't tell. But one thing we do know; you would not rewrite the poetry of the late nineteenth century. You would not go back on the experiment of modernism. You would go forward to some new kind of successful poetry.

The point I want to make, then, is that there is no alternative. If you do not like the excesses of avant-garde modernism, or the excesses of poetic barbarism, you cannot go back to writing quatrains about nature. It would be simply a bore. (In the same way, the painter cannot go back to academic painting as it was before Edouard Manet. And the musician cannot go back to so-called Classicism, except as a temporary diversion—and even then, one return is enough.) The road is forward, not backward.

The road forward is still through Modernism. Although this movement has produced masterpieces—James Joyce's *Ulysses*, T.S. Eliot's *Waste Land*, the poetry of Cummings and Wallace Stevens, and many of the Cantos of Ezra Pound—the movement has never achieved its full human and artistic development. The excesses to which it logically leads are necessary, as limits that must be tested, but one does not give up wine because some people are drunks. The real development of what we call modernism is still in the future.

The reason for this is that modernism is a great human and artistic turning-point. It is not merely a revolt against a sterile past and an indulgence in wacky absurdities. Modernism, in its essence, is the total liberation of man and a search for his deepest creative sources.

It means perpetual innovation, as this is required by the subject and the advancing conditions of the search. It means the release of personal vitality and energy for the individual.

And just as modernism means total freedom of self-realization, for the artist and the individual, it is an art powerfully engaged with society. It is profoundly revolutionary, without ideology or violence. It is eternally at war with oppression, bureaucratic tyranny, stupidity, and mere habit. It takes the hammer to the Golden Calf, and the bitch goddess, and all those substitutes for reality and spirit that stand in man's way. Because, most important of all, modernism descends to the destructive element of reality, and it tries to raise that reality, by an act of criticism, or by ecstasy, to the height of vision. (In other words, it is terribly realistic, and infinitely ideal, i.e. romantic, at one and the same time.)

This is why, despite our parlous state—or perhaps because of our state—modernism is still the way, to the full realization of art and life that we have set out to find.

NOTES

1 Andre Farkas and Ken Norris, ed., *Montreal English Poetry of the Seventies* (Véhicule Press, Montreal, 1978).

2 Quotations in the preceding three paragraphs are from Frank Davey, *From There to Here* (Press Porcepic, Erin, Ont., 1974).

LOUIS DUDEK

The Theory of the Image in Modern Poetry

The subject is a rich one, but let me open with a bold and challenging statement, putting in a nutshell, so to speak, the gist of what I have to say. It is this. Modern poetry, like all modern art, is a great fertile creative movement which contains many liberating, anarchic, destructive principles in its make-up; but there is none more devastating for twentieth-century poetry than the idea contained in Gertrude Stein's famous line usually quoted as 'A rose is a rose is a rose is a rose.'[1]

It is a line that has never much been understood. Usually it is taken for pure nonsense. When Gertrude Stein herself visited America in 1934 a student at the University of Chicago asked her what it means. She replied that 'when the language was new ... the poet could use the name of a thing and the thing was really there ...' but that now 'they [the names] were just worn-out literary words.' She said further: 'You have all seen hundreds of poems about roses and you know in your bones that the rose is not there ... But I think that in that line the rose is red for the first time in English poetry for a hundred years.'[2]

'The rose is red for the first time in English poetry for a hundred years...' All the arrogance of modern poetry is in that statement, for Gertrude Stein was certainly an egotist. And the statement isn't even true. She tells us that she wants to 'name a thing' so that 'the thing is really there.' But that is not really the point of the line 'A rose is a rose is a rose is a rose.' It does not make you *see* a rose. It says that a rose is *only* a rose.

And so it is mainly this idea in modern poetry—an idea that Gertrude Stein in no way originated and which she only re-stated in a striking (incomprehensible) way—that I want to discuss with you tonight. It says that a rose does not represent or symbolize something other than a rose; it is merely a rose. The line reiterates this statement in order to emphasize the denial of symbolic meaning: 'A rose is a rose ... is a *rose* ... is a *rose*.'

I say that Gertrude Stein did not invent this idea. She is not even an important spokesman for it. (The line, in fact, does not suit Gertrude Stein's kind of writing very well. She ought to have said 'A word is a word is a word is a word.') The important spokesmen for the idea that a thing is merely what it is are people like Ezra Pound, T.E. Hulme, Ford Madox Ford, Henri Bergson, Rémy de Gourmont; and going forward, William Carlos Williams, Louis Zukofsky, Charles Olson, Robert Creeley.

Ezra Pound is perhaps the most important formulator of the dogma, though he, too, is not the originator. As early as 1912, we find him saying, not that 'a rose is a rose,' but that 'a hawk is a hawk.' It occurs in a passage in *Poetry Review* for February 1912:

> I believe that the proper and perfect symbol is the natural object, that if a man uses 'symbols' he must use them so that their symbolic function does not obtrude; so that a sense, and the poetic quality of the passage, is not lost to those who do not understand the symbol as such, to whom, for instance, a hawk is a hawk.[3]

(You will notice that, at this stage, the symbolic meaning is still permissible. Later it will hardly be tolerated.)

The idea recurs in Ezra Pound's writing. You may know that I had a small correspondence with him in the years after 1949, now published in the book *Dk/Some letters of Ezra Pound.* Well, forty years after saying that 'a hawk is a hawk,' he wrote to me (in 1951 that 'General knowledge is from PARTICULARS'[4] (the word *particulars* capitalized); and in another letter, two years later, he repeated the same idea in three different ways: 'Katz is Katz' (meaning that a certain John Kasper is what he is, and one should perhaps allow for that); and 'leave MUS as Mus' (meaning that Mussolini is Mussolini, just what he is, 'conditioned by circs'—by circumstances —and therefore also worth making allowances for); and finally, in the same letter, a 'leaf is a LEAF'[5]—the old 'rose is a rose' principle in Pound's latest version.

In this letter, Pound expounded further on the idea as follows:

> get away from the shit of symbolism/basic CUT of imagism.
> leaf is a LEAF/that is enough/it has infinite implications
> Look at it. look at the leaf/don't try to make it into
> a symbol of something ELSE.
> (Letter received Feb. 21/53)

As you can see, we are quickly getting into the deeps of literary theory. The key phrase here was the eliptical aside: 'basic CUT of imagism' (the word CUT in capitals). This refers to the Imagist movement of 1912 and its relation to French Symbolism, as Pound came to see it by 1953. He is saying that English and American Imagism *cut out* the symbolic element, while retaining the aesthetic of imagery, contained in Symbolism. There is much to ponder in this rather brutal laconic observation: 'get away from the shit of symbolism / basic CUT of imagism.'

The history of Imagism has been plentifully written about. We have three complete books, by Glenn Hughes (1931), by Stanley Coffman (1951), and by J.B. Harmer (1975), reviewing the literary history and the theory behind this movement.

Briefly, the story is that a group of poets under the leadership of T.E. Hulme met at the Café Tour d'Eiffel in Soho in 1909 and 'talked about Image.' This was later referred to by Pound as 'the forgotten 'School of Images' of 1909'[6]

In the autumn of 1912, Ezra Pound christened the poetry of H.D. and Richard Aldington 'Imagiste'. (The most picturesque version is that reading over their manuscripts in a tea-shop in Kensington, he said to them suddenly, 'You are *Imagistes*,' thus inventing the word and the movement.) As foreign editor for *Poetry* (Chicago), he published the first poems of Hilda Doolittle over the signature of 'H.D., *Imagiste*'; and within a few months he collected an anthology of poetry which he entitled *Des Imagistes*, containing poems by himself, H.D., Aldington, F.S. Flint, James Joyce, William Carlos Williams, Ford Madox Ford, Amy Lowell and a few others. The book appeared in 1914. This was the Imagist movement, so far as there was a movement.

After 1914 the group split up, Amy Lowell seceding to form her own Imagist and free-verse movement, as distinct from Ezra Pound. She published three collections from 1915 to 1917, entitled *Some Imagist Poets*, a poetry of a looser, more verbose kind than that which Pound advocated. He called it 'Amygism', and he did not participate in these anthologies.

So the Imagist movement proper came to an end. It was referred to with faint disparagement, in accounts of modern poetry, in the decades that followed, usually with the thought that it was merely a short-lived movement—a spurious 'ism'—and that it had really affirmed some universal principles of poetry that were obvious in any case, precise use of language and vivid display of imagery. But there is more to it than that. I have always felt that Imagism held the key to modern poetics; and in recent years this view has been more and more often expressed by critics. ('Imagism is modern poetry in miniature,' says William Pratt in his little anthology of Imagist poetry.[7]) The reason is that the idea underlying Imagism has poured into the poetry of each generation that has followed the beginning of modernism. It is central because it flows from the center of our philosophical predicament and our sense of actuality. For better or worse, it lies at the heart of our problem—the problem of modern reality—and that is why I want to talk about this tradition, so central to modernism, the poetry that runs from Ezra Pound through Louis Zukofsky, and Charles Olson, to Robert Creeley, and all who are associated with these poets.

Perhaps the first thing to say is that the idea of the image in modern poetry is less important for what it is than for what it is not. There is no consensus at all among the poets and critics as to what precisely was meant by an image. Its definition ranges from the presentation of a mere visual object to Pound's rather obscure definition about 'an intellectual and emotional complex in an instant of time.'[8] Images could consist of such matter as H.D.'s classical-mythological subjects, Aldington's occasional contemporary images, Ezra Pound's archival and historical excavations, Chinese ideograms (or pictorial signs), and dream images; or simple sensual presentations like William Carlos Williams' 'Red Wheelbarrow' or 'Old Woman Eating Plums.'

T.E. Hulme in his definitions frequently emphasized the visual aspect of images—he would speak of 'recording impressions by visual images in distinct lines'[9]—while others, Ezra Pound among them, specifically rejected the visual, descriptive, or impressionistic aspect of images. It is partly because of this lack of agreement on the meaning of Imagism that J.B. Harmer in his recent history of Imagism says that the movement 'died of its own inner contradictions.'[10] One of the principal imagists, F.S. Flint, in a lecture given much later, in 1940, actually said: 'We called ourselves 'Imagists'; but the name does not matter, and in any case it was adopted as a joke rather than the challenge it finally became ... We had a doctrine of the image, which none of us knew anything about.'[11]

The source of this confusion lies partly in the history of the words *image* and *imagery*. The very word *imagination* is formed on the same Latin root: *imaginari*, to picture to one's self. Imagination is clearly the power of forming images. But what are images? The use of the word *image* in the discussion of poetry was already well-established from the seventeenth century. Dryden speaks of wishing that 'there may be in the poem any instance of good imagery.' And Boswell in his *Life of Johnson* says of a play, 'The whole of it is rich in thought and imagery.' Coleridge speaks of 'a casual illustration ... [introducing] the image of a woman, child, or bird.'[12]

As J.B. Harmer points out, 'Hobbes believed that imagination, by means of which images were created, was the reflection of visible and only of visible objects. After Hobbes, 'imagining' was taken to mean 'seeing', a process by which the content of physical vision was supposed to be brought into verbal form.'[13]

The derivation of the word is from Latin, *im-* or *in-ago*, to act, or do. The original meaning is that of *a copy*, or imitation, concretely a statue or effigy, which is also the oldest English meaning of *image*. But already in Latin the word *imago* could mean either a bust, engraving, likeness, or it could mean a ghost, a phantom, an apparition.

By the time the word is applied to literature or poetry it has come to mean something like 'the mental representation of things in the external world'. The Lockian psychology, which derived all knowledge from sense experience, reinforced this meaning for the next two centuries, and that is essentially the idea of it that dominates right into the twentieth century, although it is grossly superficial as a view of imagination and of the mental process.

For what is it that we perceive when we have an image of a past experience? There is no consensus about this, since different individuals do not imagine or 'visualize' in the same way—psychology has shown that there are vast individual differences—and we cannot really know what other people experience when they visualize. Actually only the mere surface of the mental process, as it appears in consciousness, is available to us; and the nature of imagination in its deeper levels is utterly unknown to us.

The image, therefore, is a mysterious bit of conscious experience—the flash that impinges on conscious thought and action—the rest of which is buried in the chambers of the mind or the brain. We know it as a powerful element of poetry, but we really do not know what it is. The verbal clue is only a hook to spring the process into action.

In any case, the literary tradition is correct in seeing imagery as standing at the heart of the poetic process. We may, in fact, say that the image—whatever it ultimately may be—is the molecular unit of poetry. We perceive it, and it is through imagery that we recognize the poetic gift. And the Imagist movement of 1912, in concentrating on the image, in fact isolated this essential element of poetry, and presented it for steady contemplation.

Now, I have said that the image in modern poetry is less important for what it is than for what it is not. 'What it is' is defined with some vagueness and contradiction, but 'what it is not' is maintained with great consistency, whether by the Pound group of 1912-1914 or the Amy Lowell group of 1915-1917. It is not generalization or abstractness of ideas. Images are 'concrete presentations'—of whatever—not general ideas. The French Symbolists, as we know, had rejected a poetry of ideas and replaced these with something like suggestion and verbal music. The Imagists equally rejected ideas (hence the heritage of Symbolism), but they replaced ideas with 'concrete' images, exact presentation. 'Go in fear of abstractions,' said Ezra Pound. 'Poetry ...' wrote Hulme in 1909, 'is not a counter language but a visual concrete one. It always endeavours to arrest you and to make you continuously see a physical thing, *to prevent you gliding through an abstract process*' (my italics). 'Poetry should render particulars exactly,' repeated Amy Lowell and Aldington in 1915, 'and *not deal in vague generalities ... We oppose the cosmic poet ...*' (my italics).[14]

I have always seen the Imagist movement as the thin point of an hourglass, through which the fine grains of imagery passed from the intellectual container of the nineteenth century, at the top, onto the 'heap of broken images' at the bottom, that is, the twentieth-century poem. By the bareness of the image, in this movement, and by the exclusion of ideas, the context of nineteenth century pantheism, moralism, religious concern, and what-not else, was excluded; and the ground was prepared for a new culture with new fresh-minted images.

And now, just this special concentration on the isolated image led to a new conception of the extended poem—the long poem composed completely of images. This development was of prime importance for literature, and it is the main subject of our interest tonight. It produced *The Waste Land, The Cantos,* the poem *'A'* by Zukofsky, *The Maximus Poems* by Charles Olson, and an entire literature derived from these writers, best represented by the scatterings of laconic poems by Robert Creeley. (Canadian literature also, in the last fifteen years, has been entirely dominated by this literary development.)

Perhaps the best way to explore this is to go to a prime source, to the writer who influenced T.E. Hulme more than any other did. This is Henri Bergson, especially in the psychological book *Essai sur les données immédiates de la conscience* 1904. (In English: *Time and Free Will, an essay in the immediate data of consciousness,* London, 1910.) In that book Bergson has the following sentences:

> D'où vient le charme de la poésie? Le poète est celui chez qui les sentiments se développent en images, et les images elles-mêmes en paroles, docile au rhythm, pour les traduire. En voyant repasser devant nos yeux ces images, nous éprouverons à notre tour le sentiment qui en était pour ainsi dire l'équivalent émotionel ...[15]

In this 'équivalent émotionel' you may already hear T.S. Eliot's 'objective correlative'. But here is the passage roughly translated into English:

'What is the source of the power of poetry? The poet is a man in whom the feelings develop into images, and the images themselves into words, amenable to rhythm, which translate them. Seeing these images pass before our eyes, we in our turn experience those feelings which were, so to speak, their emotional equivalent ...'

Notice now how the same idea appears in T.E. Hulme, who read Bergson assiduously. The poem, says Hulme, is 'an attempt by means of successive and accumulated images to express and exteriorize ... a central lyric intuition.'[16] (*The New Age*, Aug. 24, 1911).

The idea, here, is already a program for a new kind of poem—a succession of images—which Hulme did not live to write, since he was killed in the Great War. But Eliot wrote that poem, in 1921, and he, like Hulme, clearly described its method in the article on 'Hamlet and His Problems,' in 1919:

The only way of expressing emotion in the form of art is by finding an 'objective correlative'; in other words, a set of objects, a situation, a chain of events which shall be the formula of that *particular* emotion; such that when the external facts, which must terminate in sensory experience, are given, the emotion is immediately evoked.[17]

The result, of course, was *The Waste Land*. At the same time Ezra Pound, who had sat at the feet of Hulme in 'the forgotten School of Images of 1909,' discovered Chinese poetry and Chinese pictorial ideograms through Ernest Fenollosa, an Oriental scholar. In Fenollosa's essay 'On the Chinese Written Character as the Medium for Poetry,' edited and somewhat doctored by Ezra Pound, we find the following observation:

In reading Chinese we do not seem to be juggling mental counters [that is, abstractions], but to be watching *things* work out their own fate.[18]

This essay was published in parts, in the *Little Review*, in 1918. Soon after discovering Fenollosa, Ezra Pound began writing the *Cantos*, a long poem consisting of ideograms, images, bare presentations, where *'things'* work out their own fate.'

In other words, a method of poetry, aptly described as 'poetry of physical objects' or 'a poetry of things' emerged in the decade 1910 and after.[19] The chief modern poems of some length and having some claim to serious attention are written from this principle. It is a subject worth examining carefully.

Why should images, of *things*, acquire such prominent importance? It would seem that the entire history of western thought converges on *this moment*. All knowledge is merely knowledge of *this*. Such is the modern belief.

The idea of knowledge as the knowledge of thisness—Duns Scotus' *haecceitas*—goes back to the Middle Ages. It is actually an aspect of Thomas Aquinas' formulation of this idea, somewhat perverted from orthodoxy, that James Joyce adapted for his own use in *A Portrait of the Artist as a Young Man* and in *Ulysses*.[20] The luminosity of thisness, 'the blaze of being' which is a feature of God's creation for Aquinas, seemed to Joyce a sufficient justification for a certain kind of purely artistic procedure (without God), the brilliant evocation of realistic detail in a complex arrangement of one's own making.

The medieval scholastic disputation as to the reality of ideas, the so-called debate between the realists and the nominalists, is central to our problem. The nominalists maintained that universals, general concepts, words denoting a class of things—man, rose, apple—are merely ideas, mental counters, words that we bring to reality. The medieval 'realists' held that these concepts are realities, existences having a being in themselves, quite apart from the objects themselves and the human intellect: in other words, they were a kind of Platonist, though they were called 'realists'. Real here applies to the reality of ideas.

The modern world has chosen to believe that abstract words are mere counters, ideas. It has opted for nominalism. This came about, it seems to me, through the failure of rationalist philosophies, that is, the failure to get at truth through mere thinking, and at the same time the discovery that science and empiricism are the keys to practical advance in knowledge. Philosophers as different as Descartes, Leibniz, and Spinoza, had all attempted to work up to God's truth, like the medieval schoolmen, by the mere concatenation of logical abstract pieces of idea, called the operations of pure reason. And indeed they built up impressive systems of philosophy by this method. Descartes' *Discours de la méthode* defines the process; but Kant's *Critique of Pure Reason* brings it to a close, delivering the *coup de grâce* by defining the limits of pure reason.

The ultimate result of this kind of critique of abstract thinking, combined with a corresponding linguistic analysis and with the rise of empirical science, is the view that words are merely words, and that reality resides in the particulars of existence. Further, the empirical philosophy of Hobbes and Locke, supplemented by the scepticism of David Hume, led to a reliance on given sensation as the source of knowledge and left us with a highly critical approach to ideas about reality and the pretentions of ideas in themselves as having the power to unlock the mysteries of nature. The failure of achieving transcendental knowledge, or knowledge of God, through mere ideas, invalidated that whole area of speculation. Later, I see Romanticism as an attempt to convey some intimation of the transcendental through the work of the imagination, through emotions and intuition. The Symbolist movement in literature is the last refinement of that perception. But Modernism, with the Imagist theory at its origin, is a resolute attempt to found a poetry on actualities and to find the truth in mere particulars.

The result of this for poetry, when we consider merely the short poem, has been highly invigorating. There are first the imagist poems per se within the Imagist movement; and afterwards there is the influence of imagism, as the emphasis on images and on the particulars of perception spread throughout the poetry of the twentieth century.

Modernity, in its broadest definition, is merely a general liberation, in every possible direction; but it is also a liberation in the direction of contemporary reality, toward the reality of contemporary images.[21] For some poets the liberation is merely a license to indulge in personal expression of feeling and in trivial self-confession; for others an autobiography of the erotic; for others again, a license to broadcast opinionated pronouncements—the poetry of opinion; for others still, a liberation from all pre-existent form, making possible typographic experiments and even digression into other media, such as tape, radio, or film. All these things are modern in their way; but I think of modernism specifically as a line of technical development, in which the image is used as the basic unit in a construction kit, and certain kinds of poems emerge as developments from the central theory of the image.

The theory has generated a multitude of short poems, what Gary Geddes just recently referred to as 'the reductive principle ...' that 'predominates in this century: the single image, the epigram, the final death-bed couplet that will put the lid on, once and for all ...'[22] (*Books in Canada*, Aug.-Sept., 1979). But what is more fascinating still, for criticism, is the pursuit of what this theory of the image has done to the long poem: how it has produced an art-form with problems unique unto itself.

The philosophical theory of particulars—as the only certain content of human knowledge—and the attack on 'abstraction' as such, led Ezra Pound to compose his massive poem *The Cantos* according to what he called the 'ideogrammic method'; that is, a method derived from the Chinese ideogram or pictorial representation of words. In Chinese, most of the 214 radical characters—the Chinese 'alphabet'—of which the rest of the characters in common use are composed, consist of rough pictorial approximations of natural objects and processes, or of metaphorical extensions of these.[23] The concept of the ideogram, therefore, simply means the concrete presentation of particulars, as we have defined it here; and 'composition by ideograms', in the Cantos, means compositon by setting side by side examples of events, actions, texts, individuals—that is, images—rather than conveying a meaning by discursive exposition. Ezra Pound's subject is history, therefore, his ideograms—or samples of history—are concrete items of historical reality, taken from the Renaissance, the Middle Ages, from Chinese history, from American history, from ancient literature or history, and from contemporary life—the life lived by Ezra Pound.

The trouble with this kind of poem is that since it began by rejecting abstractions—it assumed that reality and meaning lie in the concreteness of things—it can have no effective abstract ideas to hold the particulars together: the particulars are somehow expected to stand on their own. Moreover, since people assume that meaning consists of understanding the abstract ideas to which all these particulars point, and there are no effective abstract ideas, most people will say that they cannot understand the poem. Only those who do not try to understand in this way, who are satisfied to take the particulars as particulars, will enjoy the poem.

But even this kind of enjoyment is well-nigh impossible. One tends, willy-nilly, to impose ideas on the particulars, and to see the whole arrangement as illustrative of general ideas and leading to some general conclusions—about history, society, human values.

Pound himself said that 'an order of values should emerge' from his poem. He tried to defend his procedure by comparing it to a fugue, or pattern with variations, in which certain themes were illustrated by different historical examples. But he had no coherent pattern of this kind to support the poem, and in the end it has remained a vast confusion of uncoordinated ideograms, at best expressing Pound's personality and the confused history of his troubled genius.

We can see this problem clearly if we examine any two or three ideograms from Pound's *Cantos* and see what the problem of interpretation must be. For example, in Canto VIII, Pound gives us this sample from the Renaissance, in a letter of Sigismund Malatesta to John of the Medici, dated 1449:

> And tell the *Maestro di pentore*
> That there can be no question of
> His painting the walls for the moment,
> As the mortar is not yet dry
> And it wd. be merely work chucked away
>   *(buttato via)*
> But I want it to be quite clear, that until the
>   chapels are ready

I will arrange for him to paint something else
So that both he and I shall
Get as much enjoyment as possible from it,
And in order that he may enter my service
And also because you write me that he needs cash,
I want to arrange with him to give him so much per year
And to assure him that he will get the sum agreed on.
You may say that I will deposit security
For him wherever he likes.
And let me have a clear answer,
For I mean to give him good treatment
So that he may come to live the rest
Of his life in my lands—
Unless you put him off it—
And for this I mean to make due provision,
So that he can work as he likes,
Or waste his time as he likes
(affatigandose per suo piacere o no
non gli manchera la provixione mai)

never lacking provision.[24]

We know that the theme is the situation of the artist in society, and we are being given the social conditions under which Renaissance art was made possible. But is this sample representative? Are we supposed to assume that no artist suffered the usual incomprehension and neglect? Is Pound basing a social-historical thesis upon a single case?

Well, a few Cantos later, in Canto XXV, dealing with events a mere century later (1537), we find Titian being penalized for receiving money and not delivering the painting he had promised. Obviously this artist cannot 'waste his time as he likes'. What are we to conclude about the two examples?

Then, at the end of the Canto immediately following, moving to the late eighteenth century (1777), we have a letter from Mozart, interpreted by Pound:

To the supreme pig, the archbishop of Salzburg:
Lasting filth and perdition.
Since your exalted pustulence is too stingy
To give me a decent income
And has already assured me that here I have nothing to hope
And had better seek fortune elsewhere;
And since thereafter you have
Three times impeded my father and self intending departure
I ask you for the fourth time
To behave with more decency, and this time
Permit my departure.[25]

Are we to assume that artists in that period were usually treated as that letter indicates? Or that the situation of artists became increasingly worse? A fact is a fact (if this is a fact); but which fact is representative? And if meaning resides in the particular, what does the particular tell us? In history, it is the generalization, derived from a multitude of facts, that may have some claim to validity. To produce such a generalization requires judgment and tact. Pound, however, is often opinionated, and he arranges his few examples brilliantly to support his heavily-charged opinion. The method he adopts, at the same time, is the very reverse of didactic; it is a presentation of particulars without any organizing scheme of abstract ideas. That is why any individual ideogram, like the ones we have just looked at, may be at one and the same time suspiciously slanted to support some narrow prejudice and also open to interpretation without any claim to historical validity within an order of ideas.

I am pointing out a contradiction within the Cantos. But my main purpose is to show that the method of concrete presentation, once it has rejected the responsibility for coherent thinking, can only result in a poem without coherent meaning. This is perhaps obvious, a truism as a proposition, but it has not been sufficiently seen as a source of trouble in the Cantos.

Louis Zukofsky was a disciple of Ezra Pound. His long poem *'A'*, written over a period of fifty years, between 1928 and 1976, purports to be a poetic record of a historical period and a record of the poet's mind. It contains a good deal of reference to the theory of particulars, and in the early sections it is explicitly committed to this theory:

> What struck you, as
> I think you meant, choppy in
> 'A', 13 years or so back when
> I tried hard for the fact...[26]

And it *is* choppy, jumping from fact to fact. It asserts the theory of objective particulars in the following passage, using the word 'objective' in three senses, first as a focussing lens, 'an objective', then in the sense of *purpose* and finally as referring to objective events, objects, sense experiences—'contemporary particulars'.

> An objective—rays of the object brought to focus,
> And objective—nature as creator—desire
> for what is objectively perfect
> Inextricably the direction of historic and
> contemporary particulars.[27]

Now you will see how philosophical, and dogmatic, this theory becomes—that all we know is the image, or the objective particulars of experience. These particulars have no more connection between them than the music of poetry, the words 'so that,' or 'and':

> The common air includes
> Events listening to their own tremors,
> Beings and no more than breath
>   between them
> Histories, differences, walls,
> And the words which bind them no more than
> 'So that,' 'and'—
> The thought in the melody moves—
> A line, flash of photoplay...[28]

Such an empirical atomism of disconnected realities, he says, constitutes our complete knowledge of objects:

> If you know all the qualities of a thing
> You know the thing itself:
> Nothing remains but the fact
> The said thing exists without us;
> And when your senses have taught you that fact
> You have grasped the last remnant
>   of the thing in itself.[29]

The phrase 'the thing in itself' reminds us of Immanuel Kant, but here it is the world of appearances which is called 'the thing in itself': the mere phenomenon is called the noumenon. It is Kant upside-down. The modern world, like modern science, stands without a metaphysic, There is nothing behind appearances, and only the apparent is real.

So Zukofsky sees himself as

>   bringing together facts
> which appearances separate:
> all that is created in a fact
> is the language that numbers it,
> The facts clear,
> breath lives
> with the image each lights.[30]

This philosophy, if it is a philosophy, is carried so far Zukofsky imagines that even after death, when all will be revealed, we will see nothing more than particulars:

> On that morning when everything will be clear,
> Greeting myself, despite glasses,
> The world's earth a rose,
>   rose every particle
> The palm open,
>   earth's lily,
> One will see

gravel in gravel
Stray bits
of burnt matches
Glass,
disused rubber,
Scrape heels of shoes,
and not trip,
Not that one will get, see
more than particulars.[31]

This extraordinary version of Revelation, in which nothing more will be revealed than 'burnt matches,' 'gravel,' 'disused rubber,' and 'heels of shoes'—however much in the form of a rose—in eternity—seems to me the literal epiphany of philosophical ignorance.

Louis Zukofsky's poem *'A'*, like Pound's *Cantos*, results in an incoherent jumble of images, connected by 'So what' and 'and'; the world it presents has no intellectual order. At best the poem is held together by Zukofsky's personal affections, his love for his son Paul, for his wife Celia, for the music of Bach: he would have it that it is held together by 'music'—his own voice. But this is doubtful. This kind of poem, the long poem of images, having no order of ideas to sustain it, gravitates to the personal, the images immediate to one's own experience. Ezra Pound tried to dig his images out of the archives of Europe, but he ended in the Pisan Cantos with his own immediate surroundings: the key to the Cantos is Pound's autobiography. So with Zukofsky, even history, even the past, becomes a personal reënactment. As he says in a rather prosy text:

> Fact—impels from incident to incident, because the Beginning comes only with the finish of what is Past. For one concerned with the Beginning, a portrait of what is closest to oneself to begin with is indispensable; it makes for honesty—what construction can be considered truth about the past?
>
> The relation of a veracious actor to his historic original, mask penetrated, per sonus—thru sound. Only speech transforms whatever skeleton remains of the past and conveys judgment of it to the intelligence. Try as a poet may for objectivity, for the past to relive itself, not for his living the historical data, he can do only one of two things: get up a most brief catalogue of antiquities (people become dates, epitaphs), or use this catalog and breathe upon it, so that it lives as his music.[32]

The world becomes a catalogue, by nature incoherent, and fragmented; and the thought, so far as there can be any in this kind of poem, also becomes incoherent and fragmented. We get only bits of thought. But I will leave the poem *'A'* for you to explore: most of it is drivel, and some of it very fine lyric—it is still as lyric that the imagist long poem succeeds—since music remains its ultimate criterion. Pound was a more gifted poet than Zukofsky, therefore his poem has more blazing, luminous passages of incoherent poetry than

Zukofsky's has. But if we are to get out of this cul-de-sac, we must examine carefully the premises from which this fragmentation of the world and the deprecation of general ideas proceeds.

For a final example, and one carrying to the furthest extreme the main tendencies of this modernist theory, I will just mention briefly a few salient points in the poetry of Charles Olson. The book is *The Maximus Poems*, together with the critical writings that support its procedures. Like Pound and Zukofsky, Olson is mainly 'moving among [his] particulars,' and his emphasis upon the immediate present is most emphatic and doctrinaire: 'How to inform all people how best they can stick to the instant.'[33]

One result of this, although it is not the intention of this epic and grandiose poem, is the gradual devaluation of the present and the actual. It begins as simple affirmation:

> there is no other issue than
> the moment of
> the pleasure of
> this plum,
>
> these things
> which don't carry their end any further than
> their reality in
> themselves...[34]

But it ends, as in most such poetry which aims at the epiphany of the actual, in triviality or in degradation:

> ... the plumbing,
> that it doesn't work, this I like, have even used paper clips
> as well as string to hold the ball up And flush it
> with my hand ...[35]

So that, although he says there is nothing 'the equal of / the context of / now!'—he must reject, as he rejects abstraction, the principles that give power and dignity to life:

> There are no hierarchies, no infinite, no such
> many as mass, there are only
> eyes in all heads,
> to be looked out of ...[36]

We see the irony of this in a passage in which Olson affirms the real yet denies it by his own example (which is surely the *reductio ad absurdum* of imagistic procedure):

> The real
> is always worth the act of
> lifting it, treading it
> to be clear, to make it

clear (to clothe honor
anew[37]

The curious point here is that this passage follows one in which a man named Shea, a ship paymaster, 'had stolen a crew's pay/30 or 40 years before'; and Charles Olson himself confesses to running off without paying the rent due to his landlord.

> ... we carried the books,
> clothes, lamp,
> all but the mirror
>
> down
> the three flights of stairs
>
> several trips, each step
> over the heads of him and his game
> going on
> in the basement
>
> And got away with it.[38]

It is hard to see how this will 'clothe honor anew'!

This aspect of the doctrine, that it draws us down to the triviality of particulars—and nothing more than the triviality of particulars—is familiar in the poetry of Robert Creeley, a close associate of Charles Olson, and in the poetry of scores of poets in the post-modernist movement following this line of development in poetry.

But the paradox is that such poetry, always pulled to 'contemporary particulars,' is also ambitious in the footsteps of Ezra Pound to take up the subject of history—to go for the epic. We see this in the long poem *Paterson* by William Carlos Williams, a poem which at least seeks the source of American decadence, and seeks to redeem language for poetry. That is, the poem has some meaning and direction. But Williams had echoed Pound in his doctrine 'No ideas but in things,' therefore his poem is overloaded with 'things,' without the true benefit of sustaining ideas. (As usual, we do not know, half the time, why the given materials are in the poem, or where the poem is going.) So in Charles Olson, history becomes the great obsession, and the poet makes his major bid as imagist historian.

> I would be an historian as Herodotus was ...[39]

His aim, of course, is to depict historical reality with the same rage for actuality that is applied to contemporary particulars.

> And what I write
> is stopping the battle,

> to get down, right in the midst of
> the deeds, to tell
>
> what this one did, how,
> in the fray, he made this play, did grapple
> with that one, how
> his eye flashed ...[40]

Olson, however, has no great genius for writing history, and he does not give us a vivid story—which, at the very least, historical writing must be. Like Pound, he gives us fragmentary anecdotes for which we do not have the context. Since general ideas have been debarred, it is a history, in particulars, where nothing is being said, the historical novel turned into a newspaper version of reality. Mainly it is slangy chatter, in current speech, over the imagined particulars of the American past—a low-mimetic version of history, and not at all the epic it started out to be.

Now , if only to show you the depth of philosophical perversity to which this writing can go, I will quote you a passage of Olson's prose, one in which he defines the bare objectivity of particulars. He says that—

> a thing, any thing, impinges on us by a more important fact, its self-existence, without reference to any other thing, in short, the very character of it which calls our attention to it, which wants us to know more about it, its particularity. This is what we are confronted by, not the thing's 'class,' any hierarchy, of quality or quantity, but the thing itself, and its relevance to ourselves who are the experience of it ...[41]

We note in this passage, as in a corresponding passage quoted earlier from Louis Zukofsky, that the object of sense experience is being called 'the thing itself,' reversing the Kantian equation. Where in the Middle Ages, in Kant, and earlier in Plato, the words 'real' and 'reality' were applied to the unifying ideas that hold the world together, the permanent order, to the modern mind the word reality applies only to the ephemeral and transitory, the world of the senses.

It follows therefore that Charles Olson dissents explicitly from Greek rationality and the entire tradition which descends from the Greeks. He says that 'We have lived long in a generalizing time, at least since 450 BC. And it has had its effects on the best of men, on the best of things.' He deplores the fact that 'Logos, or discourse ... has, in that time, ... worked its abstractions into our concept and use of language ...'[42] And he is intent on finding 'some alternative to the whole Greek system.'[43]

We have now seen the full implications of what I consider the central assumption of modernism, as shown in the evolution of 'mainline modernism', an assumption which is implicit in *The Waste*

Land, in *Ulysses*, and in *Paterson* as well as in the poems treated here. It is a defective theory. I will close by indicating briefly why it is defective, and why this kind of theory of particularity must be supplemented by a kind of thinking which would be the direct opposite of its simplistic and reductive tendency; that is, why we need a more profound philosophical criticism as a basis for new poetry.

A criticism of this theory must begin with the nature of language, it must proceed to a theory of knowledge, and it must provide an alternative to the reductive principle of reality we have examined. It must provide something better than Margaret Atwood's 'There is only one of everything'—a chip from the old modernist block. It must give us something better than Leonard Cohen's 'Connect nothing.'[44] It must correct the fallacy in Charles Olson's dogma—

> There may be no more names than there are objects
> There can be no more verbs than there are actions.[45]

(Actually, there are of necessity far more objects than there are names, and there can be no equation between the two, just as there are always far more actions than there are verbs, or names for actions.)

For the plain fact is that *all* words in human use—except for proper nouns, which are the names of individual objects and persons—all words are abstractions, they are abstract ideas. An apple is not a concrete word, it is not a particular apple. Even a MacIntosh apple is not a particular apple, it is only the name for a class; and there are therefore far more apples than there are names for apples. How can you say that, 'There may be no more names than there are objects'? There is no escaping from 'class' and 'hierarchy', as Olson would have it. A concrete 'particular apple' can no more be made of words than a rose can be made of blocks of wood. All the words in a dictionary are classifications and analytic elements of reality representing the products of human thought and human knowledge about reality.

This brings us to the second point: All human knowledge is made of words, it is a construct of words. Apart from pure perception and sensation, which provide the raw materials of knowledge, knowledge is a formulation in words of the relations, the unities, and the hierarchies of things and actions. This should be fairly obvious. No other creature or animal can be said to possess knowledge in the sense that man has knowledge. Or put it differently: the kind of knowledge that man possesses can only be conveyed in some form of language. That is, language itself does not *represent* reality, it gives us only an analytic series of verbal correspondences that may indeed make us remember and think of reality, but these have no more concreteness of particulars than algebra has of the things it represents. In fact, it is only by combining various levels of abstraction that we create the illusion of concreteness.

If this is true—and on close examination I think you will find it to be true—then we can go on to my concluding point. Human knowledge does not contain all of existence. Clearly, the part of reality that is contained in words, in the form of human knowledge, is but a small part of all reality and all existence. The greater part, beyond the known, is that part of being and existence which is not known—the mystery, the power, and the source of creation. We may then ask whether there is any relation between the known and the vast reality which is not known.

When I look at a tree, I see its colour and form and the magnificent display of visible parts. I know it is a maple, or elm, or a great fir; I may know a great deal more about it if I have any knowledge of trees. But I also believe that what I know and what I see has some correspondence to a greater reality, the secret source of being in that tree, which I do not know.

In the same way, all our knowledge—may it flourish and increase—has some fruitful and valid relation to that greater total existence of which we know only a small part. We must come to this with a great scepticism and a great faith. Scepticism as to the reach, and the meaning, of knowledge; and faith in the being and order of that total reality unknown to us.

A poem, of course, is partly about experience and existence as we know it. But its greater power, if it is a true poem, derives from the faint hint or suggestion it gives of that other, unknown world of being. I think of the closing lines of a recent poem by a Montreal poet, Ken Norris:

> the debris that lines the beach
> is wrack enough to fill the pages
> of every notebook I'll ever know;
> I can catalogue every rock, every crab skelton
> & still it will be incomplete.
>
> The sea's transparency
> extends only a short way out
> & then there are the secrets of deep water.
>
> The particulars are not enough.[46]

This is perhaps an important turning point. 'The particulars are not enough.' A little more in that direction and we will see that a rose is not merely a rose; a rose is not a rose, a rose is more than a rose. A rose is also love, a rose is beauty, a rose is the hidden order of things. A rose is a piece of eternity.

NOTES

1. Gertrude Stein, 'Sacred Emily' (1913) in *Geography and Plays* (New York, 1968), p. 187. Actually the line in the 'portrait' reads 'Rose is a rose is a rose is a rose' and may refer to a chap named Jack Rose mentioned earlier in the same portrait. But Gertrude Stein replied to the Chicago students as quoted, so that the popular form of the line also exists within the canon, as referring strictly to 'a rose'.
2. John Malcolm Brinnin, *The Third Rose: Gertrude Stein and Her World* (Boston, 1959), pp. 337-338. Howard Greenfeld, *Gertrude Stein, A Biography* (New York, 1973), pp. 127-128.
3. J.B. Harmer, *Victory in Limbo: A History of Imagism*, 1908-1917 (London, 1975), p. 159.
4. Louis Dudek, ed., *DK/Some Letters of Ezra Pound (Montreal, 1974), p.67.*
5. *Ibid.*, p.95.
6. Charles Norman, *Ezra Pound* (New York, 1960), p. 83.
7. William C. Pratt, *The Imagist Poem* (New York, 1963), p. 13. Cf. 'The truth is that imagistic ideas still lie at the center of our poetic practice.' Peter Jones, *Imagist Poetry* (Harmondsworth, 1972), p. 14
8. Ezra Pound, *Make It New, Essays (London, 1934), p. 336.*
9. J.B. Harmer, p. 30.
10. *Ibid.*, p. 43.
11. *Ibid.*, p. 17.
12. Quotations from NED.
13. J.B. Harmer, p. 161.
14. Quotations from J.B. Harmer, pp. 156, 155, 160.
15. Henri Bergson, *Essai sur les donnés immédiates de la conscience* (Paris, 1904), p. 11.
16. J.B. Harmer, p. 167.
17. T.S. Eliot, *Selected Essays*, 1917-1932 (New York, 1937), pp. 124-125.
18. Ernest Fenollosa, *The Chinese Written Character as a Medium for Poetry* (Washington, D.C., n.d.), p. 56.
19. J.B. Harmer, pp. 139, 168
20. See William T. Noon, S.J., -Joyce and Aquinas (New Haven, 1957).
21. See 'The Meaning of Modernism,' in Louis Dudek, *Technology and Culture* (Ottawa, 1979).
22. Gary Geddes, 'Make Ars Longer,' in *Books in Canada*, Aug.-Sept., 1979, p. 4.
23. See D.G. Wilder and J.H. Ingram, *Analysis of Chinese Characters* (Taichung, 1963). Based on Baller's Mandarin Primer, on L. Wieger's Etymological lessons, and the Shuo wen, this study of Chinese characters is not related in any way directly to Pound yet it thoroughly confirms his view of the Chinese written character—a valuable text on this troubled question.
24. Ezra Pound, *The Cantos* (New York, 1972), pp. 28-29.
25. *Ibid.*, p. 128.
26. Louis Zukofsky, *'A'* (Berkeley, Calif., 1978), p. 214.
27. *Ibid.*, p. 24.
28. *Ibid.*, pp. 26-27.
29. *Ibid.*, pp. 60-61.
30. *Ibid.*, p. 102.
31. *Ibid.*, pp. 27-28.
32. *Ibid.*, pp. 594-600.
33. Charles Olson, *The Maximus Poems* (New York, 1960), pp. 97, 143,
34. *Ibid.*, p. 42

35. *Ibid.*, p. 14.
36. *Ibid.*, p. 29
37. *Ibid.*, p. 92.
38. *Ibid.*, pp. 90-91.
39. *Ibid.*, p. 100.
40. *Ibid.*, pp. 97-98.
41. Charles Olson, *Selected Writings* (New York, 1951), p. 56
42. *Ibid.*, p. 53.
43. *Ibid.*, p. 55.
44. Quotations from Tom Marshall, *Harsh and Lovely Land* (Vancouver, 1979), pp. 168, 169.
45. Charles Olson, *The Maximus Poems*, p. 36.
46. Unpublished poem by Ken Norris entitled 'MacIvor's Point'.

JOHN GLASSCO

A Real Good Noise: The Poet As Performer

At the annual meeting of the League of Canadian Poets (May, 1977) it was reported that exactly 100 poetry recitations had been given by its members during 1976; they were held in universities, libraries, parish halls and high school auditoriums all across Canada, and were of course funded by the Canada Council. Since the League now numbers 160 members—and due to the present tidal wave of poetic genius in Canada, they are constantly growing—it is clear that the practice and encouragment of poets reading their work in public is reaching epidemic proportions.

Back in the Sixties these recitations seemed no more than an amusing novelty, a passing fad, a concession to the illiterate, not to be taken seriously. Who can forget the coffee-house poet of those days in his uniform of jeans, work-shirt, beard and granny glasses, reading—interminably and in an almost inaudible monotone—his almost incomprehensible verses? A figure of fun, you would have said. But since then, due partly to efficient and tireless promotion by the League, the figure has grown larger, cast a longer shadow, growing canny as it caught on to what its audience wanted; it learned to simplify its message, to enunciate clearly, use a microphone, vary its voice, employ gestures, play to the gallery and make its hearers laugh. Soon, and almost insensibly, the poet had become a performer.

This was already apparent at the first mammoth 20-poet recital staged by the League in Toronto in 1968. The serious poets, with their straightforward, dignified and dull delivery, made little impression. It was the showmen who stole the show. They delivered non-poems, often little more than wordless chants or humorous monologues; but these were given with such skill and brio that the horse-laughs of applause were loud and spontaneous. Exercises in mindless diatribe were even more successful, and I recall one of these which repeatedly adjured the listener to screw a long list of institutions, attitudes and people. It was the sensation of the evening, drawing shrieks and whistles of approval.

Since then, this appreciation of voiced poetry has reached the further level reported by Anne Marriott, a well-known poet now teaching creative writing in Vancouver: "I have seen students from Grade 3 to third-year university respond overwhelmingly to a b. p. nichol chant: each student chanting the name of a vegetable in a round, like 'row your boat' until the whole room is rocking with sound—gets to the oral beginnings of poetry and makes a real good noise."

This kind of total participation, while probably harmless for young children, is surely neither healthy nor desirable for the average university student, who is both highly susceptible and already semi-literate. Indeed, as Northrop Frye declares, "a 'real' or fully engaged response to art does not heighten consciousness but lowers and debases it."

But it is not difficult to trace the rationale of such a response. It stems, I should say, from the naive listener's belief that he is getting "closer" to a poem by hearing it from the poet himself. This belief seems to be on a par with the feelings of the person who believes he is getting closer, say, to the spirit of Joyce's *Ulysses* by wandering around Dublin. The truth is exactly the opposite: such "closeness" actually hinders his appreciation of the text by adulterating it with an easy, tempting and impertinent emotion. And with a living, breathing, mouthing poet facing one on a public stage, the adulteration is still greater, for not only is one listening to *him* more than to what he is saying but, as part of a crowd, one is not so much having an esthetic experience as participating in a communal one.

It is very doubtful if the interests of poetry are being served by making it a social event at all. Poetry, at any rate as we now know it, is best received in a state of isolation and tranquility through the printed page. Moreover, for such reception, the eye is vastly superior to the ear; moving faster than the voice and serving the intelligence more directly, it can also take in at a preliminary glance the shape and length of a poem, so that the mind is prepared, as it were, for the degree and kind of attention it will be called on to give; it can also re-read and meditate a difficult or obscure passage; and finally, it can master the poem's verbal music much better, for there is no doubt that the educated *inward* ear can do more with the rhythms, vowels, syncopations and stresses of any poem than the amateur human voice can hope to do.

But there is a further reason to look askance at these recitations. For the poet who recites cannot help noting that his lighter, chattier, funnier and "sexier" poems receive the most applause from his audience, and unless he is a very strong character—which most poets are not—he may find himself composing this kind of *vers de societe* rather than serious verse.

I cannot of course deny there is a great deal of a certain kind of pleasure to be had from hearing poetry well recited. The irony is that so often we discover, on reading the poem later for ourselves, it was a bad poem; we had been seduced by the beauty of its voicing, the grace and expertise of its delivery, the personality of the poet himself. Whether that pleasure was "true" is a matter for the metaphysicians. Like the pleasure of one of those young men of medieval stories who enjoys, in pitch darkness, the favors of a hideous crone while believing she is the beautiful maiden he loves, ours was, I suppose, none the less true for being founded on a similar misapprehension. But the situation in reverse is unfortunately just as true, for we all know how badly good poets can voice their best poems; only call to mind the liturgical drone of Eliot, the metronomic drought of Stevens, the frothy rant of Thomas, the breathy melodrama of Pound, all painfully immortalized on recordings; these are things we must forget.

And this raises the whole question of the poet's role in society. Should he be a performer at all? The Montreal poet Sharon Nelson has argued that "to suggest that poets submit themselves to the disciplined work on their bodies and voices which an actor does is like telling a playwright that he may not create a character he cannot, or would not, act." She then sums up the problem stating, "The job of a poet is to write poetry. The 'poetry business'—all those auxiliary activities which allow poets to get ahead, to secure jobs as writers in residence, make a little money and seduce an audience—do little to encourage fine writing."

In any case, and for better or worse, we are still in the typographic era, and our final judgments should be literate rather than audio-visual, and arrived at privately rather than *en masse.* As Nelson wryly reminds us, "Oral tradition continues to thrive among illiterate peoples," and it is a little disturbing to see its recrudescence among us now, as in the bacchanalia in Toronto a year ago at the three-day International Poetry Festival in Hart House when, according to *The Montreal Gazette*, "at the poetry reading marathon on closing night, wine, mime, lyrics, chanting, dance, howling, gurgling, touching and exploding all wove the performance and the audience together into a heightened form of life-poetic consciousness."

Such excesses, though probably self-corrective, do underline the direction that poetry recitations may well be taking: that is, toward the idea of poetry as a mindless emotional release, a kind of pentecostal "service of witness"—with the poet as priest or shaman—or, what is almost as bad, simply as pseudo-cultural vaudeville, a form of "showbiz".

RALPH GUSTAFSON

The Sequence

A poem can contain any subject. But content does not make a poem. Words do.

A poem resides in its verbal craft and of all the constructions which a poem may take, the sequence, the poem by sections, is the one, I think, most peculiarly contemporary. The architecture accommodates the modern temper. Its structure and complex of meditation, irony and extension, convey the contemporary world of incompletion and, at the same time (in accordance with Poe's injunction) maintain tension. It accommodates our imperative for lyricism, resolution (in the musical sense), comprehensible ambition, and, to the extent of these successes, supplies coherence if not inclusive unity. A further demand by this age of romantic survival is met: the structure satisfies the personal desire to shape heterogeneous experience, sublimates the need of quotidian accomplishment; it can, if it wills, serve as a chronological poetic journal, the momentum of which approaches the conceptual and physical continuity of the narrative. The sequence provides worthwhile evidence of the progress of a soul. The world is in enough fragments.

A poem is superior to the extent that the verbal music heard is the meaning; otherwise, it is prose. As an art, music has the superiority over poetry in that thought in music is sensuous. Poetry without thought is vapid. Its struggle therefore is not to become prose. In its greatest reaches it achieves the condition of music. But whatever the degree, the poem to be a poem must be rightly heard and rhythmically felt. The poet can be as non-verbally tone-deaf as Yeats was, but his ear must hear, his pulse must respond.

The sequence is close to the construction of music; at best, it achieves a nearness, almost an identity, with music. The shaping of the turmoil of contemporary experience can best be achieved by the procedures of music through which the sequence moves: the progression of exposition, development and resolution: the sonata, not only in its meaning of 'suonare', to sound, but in its transformation of suite into symphony. Movement is made through a modulation of keys in affinity, into the 'home' key; from cruel April to *shantih,* if you will, from consultation with the dead to the 'men not destroyers' who end Pound's *Cantos.* The movement, at last, being toward dominant significance. The poem structured in this way has marked our century: Eliot composing his four quartets, Stevens playing his blue guitar, Crane as Orpheus building his bridge, Pound confounding chaos with sequential counterpoint.

D.G. JONES

Preface to *Mainstream:* An Unpublished Anthology (1973)

Dear Peter,

This is a radical, challenging, fine anthology. It must meet quite a challenge after leaving out Roberts, Carman, D.C. Scott, A.J.M. Smith, P.K. Page and Margaret Avison, not to mention others still. Certainly, even on its own terms, some poems by these poets might be included, but I gather not enough from your point of view. In any case, I think your selection can meet the challenge and justify itself.

The selections have a very real integrity. What we have here is the Canadian's encounter with the earth: its gravity and variety, its fragility and endurance, its capacity to inform us and finally to digest us. It begins with Lampman dreaming in the grass and ends, at present, with an old woman under the grass. The selection achieves what Charles Mair and the nineteenth century propagandists for poetry called for, what A.M. Klein called for, a green inventory. Indirectly these poems make up a dense catalogue of particular animals and birds, particular insects, particular trees, flowers, weathers and seasons. The rhetoric of the poems is a rhetoric of particulars; whatever is said has the texture of the concrete, sensible world, a world encountered by the body. Margaret Atwood presents us with two gardens, the wild and the cultivated. The wild tends to dominate here, and call in question the cultivated, as the diction and rhythm call in question the cultivated rhetoric of ideology or technology.

One is really struck by the tenacious grip that the natural world has on the Canadian imagination, from Lampman to Layton, from Purdy to Nowlan and Newlove, Helwig and Yavorsky. George Johnston was one of the first and one of the few to make peace with the city, Lampman's Ottawa. But what you have chosen are not the urban and suburban poems, but the pastoral poems, the poems where the earth and the dark honey of the earth draws him out into Lampman's own territory—and that seems to be where Johnston himself is drawn in the later volumes. Klein, the *citadin,* was likewise drawn to the country, made of Montreal a pastoral world. And that is where the young are drawn, Wayman or Zieroth, Belford or Pat Lane. And it is in defense of themselves that Atwood and Lee defend the earth, attack the civilization they inherit.

One has a distinct sense that for these Canadians the whole political, commercial, industrial world is a dream, an evanescent nightmare, insubstantial. They build cities and invade the landscape, are violent and aggressive, but *they* are not finally real. They will eventually subside into the earth like Purdy's farms, leaving a few ripples of broken road or fence post, so many rusting Titanics under the green waves of earth.

Nature is a sea. The rational and technical structures disappear into it, as earth covers Indian bones, as fog dissolves navigational signals, the headlands and then human laughter, as the rain dissolves Layton's Laurentians and Layton himself, transforming them into a teeming green Africa. A man's eyes are like lakewater in which you can see boulders on the bottom; the boulders breath under the lake; Atwood's "I" takes refuge there, out of the picture. Layton sees the bulge of a Coke bottle, shining amber in the green grass. Another sees the moonlit glint of a beer can sinking into the earth. What is real or enduring is in that sea, lives there, as Birney's slug in the woods lives in his slow motion world on the forest floor.

The attempt to climb out, to shake the dust off one's feet, to live on the heights, in the rarified air—to do this too glibly or defiantly, leads to madness or to destruction, as in Birney's "Bushed" or "David". That is the gist of the attack on "The City of the End of Things," Toronto, America, in Lampman, in Lee, in Atwood, in Zieroth. To live in the civilized world that ignores, scorns or desecrates the landscape it passes through is to suffer the neurotic violence imaged in Paulette Jiles, to rage like Layton and get your nose busted like Acorn, to conclude with the despair of Newlove: "It is not true that we were made to live on the earth."

Their dream of earth is not sentimental. One gelds rams with one's teeth; one shoots bulls; one breaks butterflies. Souster praises the wild carrot or Queen-Anne's-Lace; Acorn the goldenrod choking out the timothy; Purdy the stunted arctic trees. Layton identifies with stunted trees climbing an exhausted hillside. Their world too is violent enough. It is no Eden; it is vivid with sex and death; with the taste above all of otherness, a real individual presence, the resistance and weight of intricate things that are not us, of a world that like the weather we cannot control and that swallows us, and which is nonetheless somehow our element.

You don't care much for Gwen MacEwen's work or for allegory.

She has a story, however, in which the central character is delighted by snow, plays a million games with the snow, finally goes naked into a blizzard of snow and dies—not because he wanted to touch the snow but because he wanted the snow to touch him. She has another story that concludes the series and in which the central character runs naked in the moonlight through the gothic arch of MacKenzie King's ruins into the wilderness that lies beyond. He wanted to be touched by the wilderness. I think of John Hornby, moving closer and closer each year to the tree line and beyond, each year with fewer and fewer provisions, less and less protection. I think of many of the poets in your anthology. They wished to be touched by the wilderness of experience, of the world outside the arched enclosures of convention. They have been touched and this is a record. It is an articulation of their touching.

That you have so consistently selected such records, your anthology may appear touched in another sense. So did John Hornby. But so must something that I believe more and more to be central to the Canadian character; this perverse desire to be touched by the other, by the arctic element in its most intimate and finally lethal being, that it makes them fools in the eyes of Promethean or technological man—in the eyes of the good Canadian banker.

As long as this dream of earth and this hunger for the naked encounter with it remains inarticulate, unconscious or underground, it will remain sinister, perverse, a crazy distorting force in our lives. A drag. It seems to me it becomes more and more articulate in the course of the years, the gradual filling up of the pages, poem upon poem, in this green inventory. It invades the city; it invades the mind, the alphabet, and the alphabet, as in Klein, begins to become flowers, pollen, sensations, the touched earth.

The desire here is not to impose an order on the world. It is to encounter the orders of the world, in the world. It implies a wholly different set of values and aspirations, a wholly different culture than that we have inherited from much of Western civilization, whether represented by Christian Europe or industrialized America —commercial and technological man. If it could become articulate in the city, in the institutions and aspirations of a large number of people, it would transform the map of our lives, and end something of the typical Canadian schizophrenia.

The attitudes of these poets can be related to the new concern for the environment, conservation, ecological awareness. But their concern goes beyond the technocrat's practical sense of space-ship earth and may finally be opposed to his aims: the exploitation and manipulation of the earth's resources for the survival and comfort of man.

Beyond the desire to preserve nature, there is a need to recognize a world beyond human influence, beyond man's capacity to preserve or destroy. The desire to live with the rest of nature and, as A.J.M. Smith remarked of Pratt and others, to *merge* with nature is more closely akin to the eastern Zen, Tao or Shinto than to western technology. But it is home-grown, and in its extreme form demands an *encounter* with the world, not for the sake of harmony, not certainly for the sake of comfort, and not even for the sake of survival, but—at the risk of death—to feel absolutely real under the touch of the *other*. The defect of Atwood's *Survival* is that survival is not our final concern. It is to be touched by reality, to be attested real.

Our reality depends on our encounter with earth. As the modern world develops we live increasingly in a physical and mental environment in which we encounter only reflections of ourselves. It is then only the man who steps out into the fields, who works on the frontiers, in the woods, in the mountains, in the arctic, who encounters something other than himself, something elemental, something that resists. To note how little respect these poets have for the more prestigious, abstract and powerful achievements of society, the world of financial, industrial and political power, is perhaps disturbing. Typical of poets, one might say. From Lampman to Newlove, the Canadian imagination seems incapable of taking these things seriously, except as a kind of sinister dream, a kind of phantasmal activity whose consequences are nightmare. No one is more ready to notice financial, political and military power than Irving Layton. Yet when Layton goes to Spain he sees Franco's regime as an ephemeral organization set against the background of the land, the movement of the seasons, of biological time. He identifies with the worms in the red earth. No one is more prepared to grasp and celebrate the large enterprises of human society, technical, commercial and ideological, than E.J. Pratt. Yet his interest lies on the frontiers of these activities where man encounters the land, the sea, the irrational virtue, courage or stubborness of man. The whole magnificent apparatus of civilization is tested at the point where it encounters the elemental. Where it comes to terms with it, as in "The Last Spike," "Dunkirk," "The Roosevelt and the Antinoe," it is successful. Where it fails to do so it disappears like a gaudy illusion as the Titanic disappears in the sea.

These are games of survival, complex and powerful. In part they may be motivated by the fear of life: the mark of Canada, says Lee. And certainly they are designed to reduce the pressure of reality, to hold out the sea. But it may be that the fear of life increases with their very success, as our increasing "security" diminishes our own sense of reality. The fear becomes the obverse of our desire: to be touched by the elemental, by the rain, wind, frost or fire—to behold reality naked as Semele beheld the naked godhead and was consumed.

For many the godhead, the pure divinity in the sky, has vanished. Much of the natural world is changeable, subject to man. The elemental is pushed to the frontiers, to the arctic barrens or the cosmic spaces. For Dennis Lee that absolute reality has become the "void." Yet he concludes his "Civil Elegies" with an appeal to the earth:

> Earth, you nearest, allow me.
> Green of the earth and civil grey:
> within me, without me and moment by
> moment allow me for to
> be here is enough and earth you
> strangest, you nearest, be home.

It is not just an appeal; it is a testimony. These poems record the encounter with earth, with the things of the earth. Their rhythms and images testify to something solid, elemental, *other* that their authors have touched, that they have been touched by. Like John Newlove, who has scared himself again and again, deliberately, in the mountains, on the prairie roads, who has said of the fear and the fear of death, we must swallow it whole and be strong, these poets have in one way or another slipped out of our various life-support-systems to make unmediated contact with the world around them. And they have confirmed its vivid reality, and their own. The poems bear the taste of that reality, which, in its detail, is a Canadian reality. And in that respect the anthology justifies its title, *Mainstream.*

Sincerely,

D.G. Jones

D.G. JONES

Grounds for Translation

"I speak of your race and mine; both were at Babel."
—Lazar Sarna, *The Man Who Lived Near Nelligan*

Ah! comme la neige a neigé!
Ma vitre est un jardin de givre.
Ah! comme la neige a neigé!
Qu'est-ce que le spasme de vivre
A la douleur que j'ai, que j'ai!

No one, I suspect, has produced a satisfactory translation of these lines from "Soir d'hiver"—unless it might be Walter Burton, the bizarre Montreal investor, poetaster, and would-be-promoter of Emile Nelligan in Lazar Sarna's novel *The Man Who Lived Near Nelligan.* Yet among the various madly inspired fragments I find no trace of "Soir d'hiver" unless it is a hidden echo in Burton's poem beginning:

In the dark pits you will find
Drama will appear as silence.[1]

"The worst fate of a poet," Burton writes to Emile, "is oblivion; it appears to me that the greatest debility facing you in writing is the language." Had Nelligan lived in France there had been no problem, but to live in Quebec, in North America, and to write poems in French is to have no audience. But, says Mr. Burton, "We will hire the finest translators and turn your work into a highly saleable commodity."[2]

Mr. Burton is obviously senile. Who but a madman would dream of turning a book of poems, of translations at that, and of Emile Nelligan, into a hot item? And where will he find the translator equal to "Soir d'hiver"?

In any case, why bother?

Why translate poetry—is it not impossible? And why translate Quebec poetry—especially the melancholy ejaculations of a hopeless teenager who doesn't know where he is or where he is going?

Tous les étangs gisent gelés.
Mon âme est noire: Où vis-je? où vais-je?
Tous ses espoirs gisent gelés:
Je suis la nouvelle Norvège
D'où les blonds ciels s'en sont allés.

As we all know, Nelligan went mad; and "Madness," says Prof. Hoffpauir* of Alberta, "is not something we should be encouraging."[3]

In a recent article, " 'Kubla Khan' and the Critics: Romantic Madness as Poetic Theme and Critical Response," Richard Hoffpauir dismisses Coleridge's poem, along with a hundred and fifty years of critical commentary, as vague, ambiguous, and incoherent. Mere suggestiveness is not a virtue. Pure musicality we might better look for in a piano. If Coleridge's poem implies anything it may be a faith in oracular inspiration, in divine frenzy, and that, says Prof. Hoffpauir, is something "experience tells us is not only wrong but destructive. Sanity and intelligent collaboration with other human beings are absolutely necessary for the continuance of civilization."[4]

What do we find in Nelligan but an almost total alienation? Prof. G.-André Vachon states that "La mélancolie, c'est *tout* Nelligan."[5] The poems are almost purely expressive, all evocation and musicality. Nelligan, says Vachon, in a comment designed to make Prof. Hoffpauir throw up his lecture notes, is the first lyric poet of Quebec—precisely because he has nothing to say.

Nelligan is not, of course, the whole of Quebec poetry. And, as Prof. Vachon notes, with evident relief, the times have changed.

Yet "Soir d'hiver" was set to music by Maurice Blackburn in 1949. And during the sixties, as sung by Monique Leyrac and others, it became almost a popular song. Behind the irony of Michèle Lalonde's "Speak White" there lies, I suspect, a grain of truth—even as she writes:

speak white
and please excuse us if in return
we have only our rough ancestral songs
and the chagrin of Nelligan.[6]

Isolation, alienation, even hallucination, are almost the leitmotif of Quebec poetry. I could quote John Glassco's translations of Saint-Denys Garneau, "A Sealed House," or "Un Bon Coup de Guillo-

---

*Prof. Richard Hoffpauir has strenuously objected to Prof. Jones's interpretation of his critical theories, and his objections are set forth in his essay "A Response to D.G. Jones's 'Grounds for Translation'" which appeared in *Ellipse* No. 22 (1978, pp 107-114).

tine," or "Accompagnement." I could quote from Alan Brown's translations of Anne Hébert, "The Small Towns," or F.R. Scott's translation of her "Manor Life," where the speaker lives in a house totally unfurnished except for its mirrors, from which a figure emerges and "Shapes himself to you, naked and thin/ And imitates love in a long bitter shiver."[7]

In John Thompson's translation of "Continuer à vivre" Roland Giguère writes, among other things:

> we felt like viruses
> gaping wounds
> pus poison wounds
> rank blood and wounds
> when certain words rose and went putrid
> on our raw cracked lips
>
> . . . .
> and to go on living
> in our isolate silent cells
> we began to invent a world
> with the forms and colours
> we had dreamed for it[8]

The more we read the less Nelligan sounds eccentric, the more his melancholy voice echoes a collective voice. And we begin to glimpse some of the motives for this voice. They include—could Walter Burton have been less mad than we supposed?—an isolation, an alienation, rooted in language.

In C.R.P. May's translation, Gaston Miron writes that he is:

> Lost, like so many of my people
> Unable to speak my language other than amongst my own folk,
> My language, mirror of our distress and our disarray
> And soon to be the mirror of our common grave ...[9]

In Gladys Downe's translation, Yves Préfontaine writes:

> I live in a land where cold has conquered
> green things, reigns grey and heavy over
> phantom trees.
>
> I am a silent part of a race that shivers in
> its sleep under frost-bound words, whose frail
> quick speech is fading.
>
> I am a part of a cry all around me
> stone cliff with no language
> steep cliff
> bare blade in my winter heart

My country is quietly strangling under a snow
of fatigue

Yet I go on dreaming dreams
persist in speaking,
but the wound has no echo,
for the daily bread of a race is its speech
and no light comes from rotting grain.[10]

In Malcolm Reid's translation of *The Sign-poster Howls,* Paul Chamberland speaks of the rumble rising daily from Quebec as simply a bad novel, a stupid movie, continuously playing in the movie house of America, "with nobody watching nobody interested any more in comprehending / the torment of my land / its anguished face iced-in with inhibitions slashed with darkness drugged with license."[11]

That, in effect, was just what Robert Guy Scully meant when he said in Washington only last month that Quebec does not exist— that it would go on being "a non-group, a country of cripples. Alternately humiliated, frustrated, tired or wildly optimistic, frenetic and foolishly ambitious," that while some might escape, "Behind the glass wall fear and insane dreams go on building as before."[12]

Ah! comme la neige a neigé!
Ma vitre est un jardin de givre.
Ah! comme la neige a neigé!
Qu'est-ce que le spasme de vivre
A tout l'ennui que j'ai, que j'ai!

Why, Prof. Hoffpauir might ask, after generations of near perfect resistance, should English-Canadians have lapsed from sanity and begun translating so many expressions of despair and madness?

It is time for an interlude.

In my mouth I taste the honey of your mouth and of
my body in yours
O unexplored land, my strange beautiful one, new to
this love, your arms whose name I have not yet
found
are around my neck like the night, rich with women,
the rulers of this unknown country
No do not speak, let the air bring your breath
to my lips
Don't speak, sigh only, be my captive bird
and my silence rests in your eyes like an unfamiliar
body
I revolve in the depths of your eyes
I wander, I search for you,

I prowl in your hair's gold aureole
I loose myself in you, O soother of men, O shelter
    of love
I die in you, I no longer have any face, only your
    face
and now you shudder and die also in me
You no longer exist I no longer exist   we are
We arrive together we are renewed[13]

That was "Awareness" by Jacques Brault, translated by Margaret Atwood and Charles Pachter.

Experience I think tells us there is something wrong with the idea that poetry is untranslatable—or, if not wrong, naive—as with the idea that poetry, like any utterance worthy of our attention, must prove in the final analysis to be exemplary, rational, something to be judged in terms of "efficient communication." If poetry were like this, I presume it would be essentially translatable. The many voices to the contrary suggest it is not.

Prof. Hoffpauir's article betrays an enormous anxiety in the face of vagueness, ambiguity, radical paradox or contradiction, any real indeterminacy. Texts showing advanced symptoms of such a disease are to be declared minor or pernicious, dismissed or reduced to silence. A poem for Prof. Hoffpauir is, or should be, univocal.

Many who argue against the translation of poetry, while they may not share Hoffpauir's other assumptions, also assume that a poem is univocal. That is, it will afford to any number of ideally prepared, attentive and acute readers a single precise reading.

It is possible, however, that none of these assumptions is valid. Certainly much recent critical discussion suggests they are not, though I suppose Prof. Hoffpauir does not care to listen to such discussions any more than to "Kubla Khan" or various Romantic theories of poetry.

I presume he doesn't care to listen to Levi-Strauss arguing that culture is normally a sort of *bricolage,* an often fantastic *analogical* resolution of views and images of man and his world. I presume he doesn't care to listen to Kenneth Burke maintaining that a poem is not a logical message but a dramatic gesture or symbolic action. Or to Harold Bloom claiming that the work of even the greatest writers, especially the work of the greatest writers, is a more or less deliberate mis-reading of their predecessors. Or to various "pluralists" arguing that the interpretation of any work will vary with the aims, terms and point of view of the critic. Or to the "de-constructionists' like Jacques Derrida or J. Hillis Miller, who claim flatly that in Prof. Hoffpauir's sense of the word no text is readable.

No text can be free of radical ambiguity, equivocation, indeterminacy. Since a word only finds its meaning in relation to other words, as used by the writer, by his contemporaries, by his predecessors, the pursuit of its potential meanings ramifies out through the whole history of language and culture. It leads into a semantic abyss; no single meaning is ever final, no single interpretation. Often, if not as a rule, one may discover that the word, like the text, contains its own contradiction. In one of Miller's examples, a "host" may be also a "guest," and the "host" or "guest" may be not only a gift-giver in the usual sense but the death-dealer, not only a friend but an enemy (the "hostis"), and the "host" may not only furnish meat and drink but be himself eaten and drunk. "The poem," Miller concludes, "like all texts, is 'unreadable,' if by 'readable' one means open to a single, definitive interpretation."[14]

Something very like Miller's point was made by Octavio Paz, here translated by Claude Esteban:

> Il n'y a pas de paroles originelles: chacune d'elles est la métaphore d'une autre qui l'est d'une autre encore, et de la sorte toutes, successivement, sont des traductions de traductions.[15]

Translation, says George Steiner in *After Babel: Aspects of Language and Translation,* is part and parcel of all discourse, that between languages being in no way essentially different or more problematical than that which takes place within a language—when we read a Shakespearean play, interpret a text by Charles Olson, attempt to pin down a government paper on language policy or struggle to understand one another in our daily exchanges. Every speech act moves away from the conventional norm towards a particular dialect, slang, jargon or idolect. We communicate with a wink or a shrug, with irony or polite formulas, often to conceal as much as to reveal. Babel, the fantastic proliferation of language—190, says Steiner, listed for Mexico and Central America alone—points to a drive quite the opposite of that towards "efficient communication." Outside a few highly specialized and circumscribed areas the demand for transparent, unequivocal, univocal utterance is bound to be frustrated. Says Steiner:

> The tensions between private and public meaning are an essential feature of all discourse. The hermetic poem lies at one extreme, the S.O.S. or the roadsign at the other. Between them occur the mixed, often contradictory and to some degree indeterminate usages of normal speech. Vital acts of speech are those that seek to make fresh and 'private' content more publicly available without weakening the uniqueness, the felt edge of individual intent. The endeavour is inherently dualistic and paradoxical. But if we listen closely, there will not be a poem, not a live statement from which this 'contradictory coherence' is absent.[16]

The poem may resist translation more than many other kinds of utterance. It is no doubt true the translation of a poem from another language will always be a mis-translation; it is, inevitably, one interpretation. But so is any reading of the poem. *Traduttore, traditore* loses much of its force when we might equally say, "To read is to mis-read." Some readings like some translations are more convincing, but none can give the lie to all others. It is a mistake to assume that we can arrive at a final, definitive interpretation. And rather than dismissing a text when it fails to yield one up, as Prof. Hoffpauir would have us do, we can only go on listening closely to any text that promises us some real if contradictory coherence.

Further, where Prof. Hoffpauir is aghast at the suggestion that a poem might legitimately beguile us into believing a falsehood, that this might even be called an essential profundity, Prof. Steiner declares:

> My conviction is that we shall not get much further in understanding the evolution of language and the relation between speech and human performance so long as we see 'falsity' as primarily negative, so long as we consider counter-factuality, contradiction, and the many nuances of conditionality as specialized, often logically bastard modes. *Language is the main instrument of man's refusal to accept the world as it is.*[17]

Nelligan would have said aye to that.

We live by a strange dynamic: to communicate, to translate, and to produce the untranslatable, to cultivate silence. But, if it is true that Babel may be our secret delight, that mankind may indeed have been kept vital and creative by being scattered among tongues so that there is in every act of translation, as Steiner notes, a touch of treason, it is equally true that we delight in sharing our most intimate secrets, that we must speak and be heard, listen and translate, or go mad. A wholly non-verbal intercourse with the world may sustain the odd solitary or saint, but most people left in solitary for any length of time start talking to themselves; they become "bushed" or go "loco" or start to hallucinate. It is not sanity and intelligent collaboration that are necessary to civilization, as Prof. Hoffpauir tells us, but civilization that is necessary to sanity—civilization as world of discourse in which people speak to each other, listen and translate.

Quebeckers more than most have suffered the effects of bowing to the idols of civilization while being deprived of the benefits of real civilization. The burden of much Quebec poetry has been precisely that nobody has been listening. When Crémazie's old soldier goes to the Court of France after the Conquest to appeal to the king, he finds himself in much the same position as Joe Clark trying to get an audience with Giscard d'Estaing; nobody listens. Even the dead in his "Promenade de trois morts" find no audience—in Heaven, on Earth, or in Hell. Nelligan wrote that he was one of those "Qui n'a pour l'écouter que l'oreille des morts."[18] As Chamberland put it, nobody cares, neither the French, nor the Americans, nor the English-Canadians, nor the local authorities, nor even, perhaps, the neighbours. Jean-Guy Pilon calls the Quebecker "L'Etranger d'ici," of whom he writes in F.R. Scott's translation:

> He came from a country of devout pirates
> Where indifference was taken for dogma
> The idiot for master
> The sick man for the seer
>
> It was a country of useless struggles
> And magnificent ruins
> A country eaten by vermin
>
> When he wished to cry out his rage
> They would not allow it
>
> They hardly allowed him to die.[19]

It was that same old indifference that stung Robert Guy Scully into saying the things he did in Washington. And though things have changed, somewhat; though we have heard not a few shouts of rage, and even of joy; though M. Morin may find a ready ear in Paris, Scully's main point remains absolutely true and perennially relevant. I quote at length.

> Living nowhere for two centuries has a depressing effect on the life of a community. Everyone knows people need to belong, need to be part of a group. French-Canadians definitely do belong to each other. They wouldn't have lasted otherwise.
>
> But Americans, who are wonderfully alive, who are a big rich group, may not realize that groups need to belong also, belong to each other; that some grow prematurely old, tired from not being heard, from talking to themselves.
>
> French Canada has always been on the receiving end. When France or America or another country has something to communicate to the world, to the other groups, be it a new idea or a new hero or a new invention, whenever, in fact, they have love to give, they are sure to be heard and the love is sure to be returned. . . . But whenever my people have produced something, when the time comes for them to give their love, or to contribute something and be loved for it, they have hit an invisible glass wall, like the dog in the petshop window.
>
> That thin, subtle, but strong wall separates the groups that exist from those that don't. We do exist in our own eyes, but living things can't survive in a vacuum, which means you have to exist in the eyes of others.[20]

Two decades ago Roland Giguère wrote the following lines, here translated by John Thompson:

life lived between walls takes on the mask of defeat
if in some crack there isn't a gleam of hope
the hope for love the hope for freedom
the hope that in time we will live all of us live
for love[21]

Why do we translate Quebec poetry? Because, in a sense, we have been asked to. It is an immediate response to the cry to be heard, to be recognized, to be given existence in the eyes of others.

And who is going to listen if English-Canadians do not, the people who have shared the same geography, the same history, who have been "host" and "hostis", friend and enemy, for over two centuries?

The competition for attention in the world family has become more severe even as it has become more necessary. Good will, intelligence, even excellence may not earn it.

I know of myself that I did not read Derek Walcott's poems until I arrived on his island. I did not read Aimé Césaire until I arrived in his city. I did not read even such an extraordinary writer as Octavio Paz until I met him in Toronto—until his became an immediate personal voice among the dozens, hundreds, that every year claim attention. And I did so then thanks to his translators.

Without what Prof. Steiner calls trust, or at least real interest, little in the way of genuine translation or even recognition is likely to occur.

I've seen an American reviewer, a Prof. of Humanities, dismiss Paul-Marie Lapointe's poetry, or my translations, with an irritated reference to the overly lush or fetid eroticism of two lines.

On the other hand, as first the translator and then the poets read their work, I've seen an audience in Pittsburgh come alive to Paul-Marie Lapointe and Gaston Miron, so that for a few hours at least Lapointe and Miron and, indeed, Quebec existed on the banks of the Monangahela.

The recognition that occurred that evening may have slightly altered the world of the audience. I suspect it altered Miron's conception of his poem "La marche à l'amour" and even of himself as a poet, confirming that he was not, as he has sometimes claimed, a poet of Quebec only. As Robert Guy Scully would say, he had love to give, his love of Quebec, his love of woman, his love of the world, and patently, this love could be shared.

To share one's existence with anyone, in Pittsburgh or Paris, in Perth or Peking, is marvellous. But for most of the writers from Nelligan to Desrochers, from Anne Hébert to Nicole Brossard, such an opportunity will be rare. It is both more normal and more necessary to exist in the eyes of one's neighbours, in Montreal or Toronto, in Edmonton or Fredericton, in North Hatley or North Bay. And translation can become only more necessary to this end as Quebec becomes more solidly unilingual.

If we translate Quebec poetry so that Quebeckers may exist, we do so as well so that we may exist. Any genuine intercourse is reciprocal, reinforcing our existence, providing a heightened and more articulate sense of our own identity—of one's self and the other. Nor are English-Canadians possessed of such a large and assured identity that they have no need of such reinforcement.

Even as Walter Burton busies himself to discover, as he puts it, whether "Emile exists," his own sense of identity is profoundly shaken. He writes, in Saint-Jean-de-Dieu, "I am left with the impression, especially in the ward, that English is actually the little-used language of an ancient jungle tribe. The years I have spent cultivating estates and developing enterprises are abruptly made to appear as both irrelevant and undesireable. In a word, Emile makes me feel lost."[22] The ultimate irony of Mr. Sarna's novel is that Emile Nelligan exists—even in Toronto—while Walter Burton does not—even in his home town, even in his own household.

The very fact that English-Canadians share a language with the British or the Australians or the Americans may be more insidious in its affects than if we spoke French, providing the illusion of an identity made articulate by other people out of traditions and experience that are not in fact ours.

That, says Dennis Lee in "Cadence, Country, Silence: Writing in Colonial Space," is precisely what happened to him and to many English-Canadians. And when he became aware of it he discovered that his identification was less with Americans than with Quebeckers, that it was with Gaston Miron he shared the acute problems of how to live and write when you do not appear to exist, or where your existence, first in the eyes of others, finally in your own, is an illusion.

This theme is central to Lee's "Civil Elegies," where we also discover one of the most complex and significant encounters between a Quebecker and an English-Canadian yet to occur, that between Lee and Saint-Denys Garneau. Garneau and his writing exist, are alive, in Lee's imagination and his work. Lee recognized in Garneau his own nausea in regard to modern technological culture, his own thirst for the divine, his own temptation to pursue it into the void. Garneau's example clarifies such an option, dramatizes some of it's potential implications, so that Lee can both sympathize and yet reject such a course. So that he can finally write:

And now across
two decades and two nations de Saint-Denys-Garneau, my blessed, stricken
original still haunted by the
space between your ribs, maker and friend and comfortless, my
lone heroic starter, out of my own wrong start I
keep my distance and praise.[23]

Lee's profound identification within difference was facilitated, I suspect, by John Glassco's translations. But it is itself a kind of radical translation, involving all four phases of what Steiner sees as the complete "hermeneutic motion," trust, invasion, incorporation, and restitution. Garneau lives on in Lee. There is here a mutual recognition and reinforcement, a mutual giving, of one's self, of one's life, of one's love.

As Prof. Miller would say, in such an act of translation the original poet and his poem is the host, who is then eaten and digested, consumed and incorporated in the new body of the translation, of the translator, who now becomes the host within whom the original lives on, transformed.

Translation, we might say, is like sexual intercourse: it may be an expense of spirit in a waste of shame, or it may be a kind of death and resurrection into a new and larger life.

In this more profound sense, neither a translation nor a poem aims as "efficient communication" so much as at effective communion.

Nelligan's "Soir d'hiver," and how many other poems, does not aim at communicating his isolation, his despair, his existential poverty, so much as it aims at effecting just such a communion. His emptiness is highly unpleasant, negative, ugly, as Nelligan felt himself so often to be ugly—venal and mortal—in the eyes of all those to whom he would give and from whom he would receive love, be it his mother or his Muse, his "Beauté cruelle" or his "Amour immaculé." That is all he has to share, however, all he is—except that within the poem he may transform that ugliness into something beautiful, an acceptable gift of himself and his love.

To write poems, to translate poems, is to engage ourselves in the kind of intercourse that is the essence of civilization—that is the bread and wine of our existence. I have said we translate so that we may exist, so that our particular identity may be recognized and reinforced in each other's eyes. But finally we do so that we may cease to exist, so that we may say with the lover's in Jacques Brault's poem:

You no longer exist I no longer exist   we are
We arrive together we are renewed

Roland Giguére speaks of the need for freedom as well as for love. Can there be love without freedom -- the freedom to escape from our particular, limited, separate identities, as defined by our self-image, by our group and class, by the inherited culture of our society as it is codified in the language itself, in everything we read or say?

If one of the main impulses of each individual, each group, each culture, is to articulate and consolidate a definitive image of man and his world, there is an equal and opposite impulse to refuse any such definition as final. Geoffrey Hartman quotes Nietzsche as saying, "Nous avons l'art pour ne pas mourir de la vérité."

Though literature may serve, as for Prof. Hoffpauir, or Horace, or Philip Sidney, to dramatize and disseminate the existing myths and values, *la vérité*, of a particular society, it lives—secretly or openly—in revolt against any claim that the truth has been spelled out, once and for all, that everything's been said. In this respect it is not at all an instrument of clarification, of efficient communication, confirming or completing the existing structure of meaning. "L'art," writes Prof. Hartman, "ne s'ajoue pas au mode des significations; il fait de la place dans la signification même."[24] It seeks to stall, to frustrate the completion of any final sentence, to put off or prevent cultural closure.

No doubt, like the two sides of a coin, these two impulses are both basic and perennialy operative in any culture, giving it too its "contradictory coherence"—though at any moment one may receive greater emphasis than the other.

John Robert Colombo's *The Great Wall of China* views the wall as something negative, the creation of a defensive, limiting, closed society. Jacques Godbout's translation, *La grande muraille de Chine,* views the wall as something positive, the creation of a protective, nourishing, progressive-conservative society. The two versions reflect, I presume, the longstanding biases of English and of French Canada within the context of their particular game of heads or tails. And yet, we may note that Godbout's very translation manifests the more open and adventurous spirit that Colombo's original championed. It claims the freedom to play with what is given, to reverse what is given, to transform and recreate. It claims the freedom to mis-translate.

It is precisely through translation, that is, inevitably, the mis-translation, the mis-reading, that the poet, the writer, all of us who share an articulate culture, manage to find nourishment, manage to avoid being locked in "the prison house of language." As both Hartman and Miller remind us, the American poet Wallace Stevens was acutely aware that we must claim this license as the ground of any delight or life in language, of his lines, which might well have been addressed to Nelligan, or Garneau, or Miron or Chamberland or Préfontaine:

> Natives of poverty, children of malheur
> The gaiety of language is our seigneur.[25]

Let me bring the matter home in a final example. Gladys Downes takes André Major's love poem "Quel feuillage" and calls it "Words". She takes the first verse, which in the original reads:

> ce que l'on dit enlacés
> saigne comme une mémoire
> et nous tient effarés dans un rêve trop beau[26]

and she translates it as:

> When we lie together as leaves enfolded
> our words are sharply beautiful
> and hold us, shaken,
> in an amazing dream[27]

She then takes the first line and, publishing a volume of translations and her own poems, entitles it *When We Lie Together*. Here in a nutshell lies the essential process and the raison d'être of both poem and translation.

NOTES

1. Lazar Sarna, *The Man Who Lived Near Nelligan* (Toronto: Coach House Press, 1975), p. 61.
2. *Ibid.*, pp. 151-152.
3. *English Studies in Canada*, Vol. II, No. 4 (Winter, 1976), p. 408.
4. *Ibid.*, p. 420.
5. *Nelligan*, ed. Ethier-Blais (Montréal: Le Cercle du Livre de France, 1969), p. 105.
6. *Ellipse No. 3*, p. 25.
7. F.R. Scott, *St-Denys Garneau/Anne Hébert* (Vancouver: Klanak Press, 1969), p. 37.
8. *Ellipse No. 2*, p. 17.
9. *Ellipse No. 5*, p. 27.
10. "Country to Let," *The Poetry of French Canada in Translation*, ed. John Glassco (Toronto: Oxford University Press, 1970), p. 238.
11. *Ellipse No. 8/9*, p. 21.
12. *Montreal Star*, April 16, 1977, p. C-1.
13. *Ellipse No. 7*, p. 13.
14. "The Critic as Host," *Critical Inquiry*, Vol. III, No. 3 (Spring, 1977), p. 447.
15. *Le singe gramairien*, tr. Claude Esteban (Geneva: Skira, 1972), pp. 25, 28.
16. *After Babel: Aspects of Language and Translation* (New York: Oxford, 1975), p. 205.
17. *Ibid.*, pp. 217-218.
18. Nelligan, *Poésies complètes* (Montreal: Fides, 1952), p. 172.
19. *The Poetry of French Canada in Translation*, p. 189.
20. *Montreal Star*, April 16, 1977, p. C-1.
21. "Life Outfaced", *Ellipse No. 2*, p. 15.
22. Lazar Sarna, *The Man Who Lived Near Nelligan*, p. 71.
23. Dennis Lee, *Civil Elegies* (Toronto: House of Anansi Press, 1972), p. 54.

24. "La voix de la navette", *Poétique*, No. 28, (1976), p. 412.
25. "Esthétique du Mal", *The Collected Poems of Wallace Stevens* (New York; Alfred A. Knopf, 1954), p. 322.
26. *La poésie canadienne*, ed. Alain Bosquet (Montreal: HMH, 1966), p. 270.
27. *When We Lie Together* (Vancouver: Klanak Press, 1973), p. 24.

TOM KONYVES

Videopoetry

I have come to gradually surrender my poetic powers to a medium which devours words much like fire devours paper.

Screening tapes made earlier at a reading, I became aware of a certain "power" which actually transformed the poet to performer, then attempted to "putrefy" the experience into a neatly-framed (silent as the ages) fossil. The lack of a cohesive poetic experience on the screen not only created doubts about my own poems but forced the resolution to discover why certain things "worked" while others did not.

I screened 15 hours of poetry before putting together the hour-and-a-half production *"Poetry On Tape"* (1977) which included Steve McCaffery, Anne Waldman, Stephen Morrissey and Pat Walsh, and *Drummer Boy Raga: Red Light, Green Light* a six-poet 'collaberration'. By the time I began recording readings myself, I had an inkling of what I was looking for.

Screening, in the terminology of video production, is the ritual one succumbs to like the repeated chants in the Koran—simplistic repetition. (We all know the value of repetition as a purgative and proof of faith.) Two immediate observations: the poet on the screen was less effective than 'real life' and the camera could (a) refuse to participate, (b) choose to collaborate and even (c) dominate. Video had the propensity to render poetry as recital, extremely static. The best became revealed as sudden bursts of energy. An hour-reel was yielding about five minutes of sustained energy.

The printed word was looking more and more like a secret message sent from room to room, from the poet's den to the reader's bedchamber. In other words, a certain immediacy was lacking. Readings attempt to restore a missing link—the voice—while audio and video recordings wish to create a new immediacy, albeit an artificial one.

The printed poem faces no great obstacle as audio and video-poems do. Radio and television have no offshoot comparable to the small press which actually "sells" poetry in limited but consistent quantities to an audience who appreciates pale covers and neat stanzas, delighting in well-groomed dogs and math textbooks.

Taped recordings and records (discs) of poetry, although few, are dedicated to preserving "classics" first and foremost. Experimental works comprise a very small portion of available tapes and records. Their contribution to the craft has been, to be fair, infinitissimal. The past 25 years have attempted to restore sound to words but the results seemed to confirm the role of print as the 'natural' medium rather than what english profs declare perfunctorily to their students: poetry was oral in its state of innocence. Poetry has become so that, as art proper, the book has become the indwelling of its soul.

But the hare of technology never sleeps, he's just recharging his batteries. Radio and television believe in poetry only as far as the next ad. Poetry is rejected as viable programming mainly because of the market in its "own" field: if poetry books don't sell, poetry doesn't sell.

It is alarming that there is a little bit of poetry in everything but by no means is there a little bit of everything in poetry. The state of the art is in crisis.

When your own medium rejects you (newspapers used to publish a poem a day), like any business, you change or die. Poemists have sanctified the 'personal revelatory' nature of poetry and consigned it to 'book' form. For books will always be there . . .

Poetry has been more than welcome in theatre (Beckett) music (Dylan) film (Cocteau) and the visual arts (Johns) . . .

Children hear before they see, hear words before they see words and see words before they spell words (badly). And reading permits rereading, which distorts the true unfolding of the poem. Tape sheds the binding cords of decipher-by-participation, turn-back-the-page-before-continuing poetry experience one becomes accustomed to. (A New York poetess distributed mimeographed copies of her poems before her reading. Reading them (with her) gave me the feeling of pissing in the sea. Listening to her wasn't that great, either.)

Writing for video should be easy enough. It is more malleable than print or audio-tape. A good poem on tape will use all technology has to offer, repetition, dubbing, music mix, unexpected periods of silence, untranslatable sounds. "Special effects" will be the vocabulary of this new poem.

"It's interesting, but it's just not poetry." Yet the tape-recorded poem is as far advanced now as printing was when poems were handwritten. Print is by no means at an end. But its usefulness, in our sphere, is diminishing.

What then of print?

The role of print should be the scoring of a performance. The poem, as we know it, is the monologue of a poetry theatre.

Collaboration is increasing, but monologues abound. In print, mind you, not video. Access is easy enough, technical know-how takes time and patience, but after that the medium is limitless.

Some "monologues" are so fascinating that many poets never transcend 'recitals'. But the one-voice-theory is a limitation today's poet must beware of. In a poetry theatre, what we know as the poem serves two purposes—sings a plaint to divert the audience or paints a scene or object. Video allows poets to see their roles more clearly, and it is to this end I strive. Whereas I consider a line the unit of poem-making, like bricklaying, in video we substitute visual lines for printed lines and proceed to "layer" a poem: spoken words (the poet-performer); words heard (taped, dubbed); and seen (signs, subtitles, printed, painted). Naturally, a poem written with these three forms of word-smithing is never 'itself' until it is meshed with visual imagery (close-ups, cuts, dissolves, pans). If the end-product demonstrates a "judicious" mix of the two (even an interesting interplay) the poem will have a texture we will all admire.

Bad video is as possible as bad poetry. A poetry theatre attempts to take a stance somewhere between the documentation of a poem and creating a poem of dialogue, music and visual effects. The poetry, the words, should be the real motion of the piece. The other media will ultimately give way to this language.

Poetika:

With words.
The bard writes down what he sees, he looks at it, he is pleased. He is not pleased. He changes something. Something changes. The printing press appears, the poems are read, reread, recited. Books bind the bard's breath. The line is born, and will never die. The line is: never say die.

p

Narrative poetry endures until it grows old. The poetry of the last hundred years is essentially the fetching of this and that for the old man. Eventually, he dies or he is laughed at. He is buried in the book, his soul the indissoluble lines. Words follow one another like sheep.

the word sheds

The poet's response to industry and technology: the simultaneous. Ideals lose their I's. Poets begin to experiment, peering into the future. Few want it. Blake's illustration: man leans ladder against the moon. Caption: I want! I want! (1793)

communi^a_ction

The poem which most reflects our time is one whose words are in action. On the page they suggest action.

treal

The poem which most reflects our time is one whose words are inaction. On the page they suggest inaction. The value of the poem is directly proportional to the degree to which it represents action or inaction.

Tom Konyves

Having written and published poems for magazines, books, broadsides... having been there at the attending ritual of their recitals, performances... I have been increasingly setting my sights on visual media for exhibiting my poems. Video has been more accessible and pliable, too. Advantage: unfolding the poem at my convenience. Disadvantage: less freedom and rumination by the audience.

oetry changes.

Many, including myself, believe that once the suggestiveness of words becomes realized in images, there is a tendency to demystify the poem. The selection of imagery is the instrument bequeathed to the modern poet. In view of the abundance of new books of poetry, it is becoming evident that not many wish their poems to leap off the page into another element. The page has not been exhausted, they cry. Fish out of water. Out of their element. But the metamorphosis has already begun. Words have been removed from their linear context, juxtaposed to create visual excitement; syllables, letters have been isolated for their visual properties. These experiments culminate with the poem leaving the page for other "new" means of presentation. The poem is looking for a new home. The chairs are weak, the walls are peeling. The poem becomes a "free subject", its own subject, the poet disappearing like clouds of dust in cartoons. If the poem is a window, the landscape is changing. Let us change with it, let us not restore the old conventions.

picture=1000 words

It has been revealed to me that the poem is fragile and cannot sustain narrative without collapsing in a heap. This is necessary. It must then be coaxed into opening its eyes, but only for a few seconds. Dreaming follows, abruptly halted by the telephone. As it gives, it must take. Who is taking?

IRVING LAYTON

Foreword to *The Tightrope Dancer*

When I was just starting my career as a poet, someone told me that there were only two subjects worth writing about, sexuality and death. I didn't understand then what he meant, but I do now. The poet, either through genes or genius, is poised on a rope stretched tautly between sex and death. The major poet dances on the tightrope; the minor poet walks warily across it. The non-poet or poetaster, rapidly becoming one of this country's major home-grown products, doesn't even make a try at either. The literary scholar and the critic remain, of course, solidly and securely on the ground, fussily adjusting their binoculars and peering intently through them, once they have found what they believe is the right focus for watching the performance on the tightrope.

Someone else said, "When writing a poem, get the first line, get the last line, and bring the two together as soon as you can." This excellent advice has made me want to avoid the rant and rubbish taken for poetry by those perennial *culturati* whom poets in every age must contend against: the faddish, the foolish, and the ignorant. For me, poetry has meant packing maximum meaning and intensity into every line; if possible, into every word. A poem should resonate in the mind and heart long after it has been heard by the ear. Anything else, whatever my lapses in practice, I've always considered rhetoric or journalism; or short stories arranged vertically on the page, easy to read and even easier to forget. A poem, when you are done with it, must be able to get off the page, turn the door-handle, and walk directly into the lives of people.

Poetry, whatever form it takes, is an arrangement of words whose vitality endures from generation to generation. Since this is an age of atrocity, when sadists and torturers proudly wear their decorations at public functions; when terrorists who gun down helpless women and children are hailed as heroes; and when thugs and despots are listened to politely as they expound their views on human rights, it is difficult for the true poet to restrain his pity and contempt for the human condition as it is revealed to him in the present century—

difficult for him to write for human beings who accept the enslavement and murder of others without protest or execration.

Perhaps the poet's tightrope is not stretched between sexuality and death, but between love and loathing for the human race. Lacking the assurances of the theologian or the smugness of the logical positivist, the poet finds that this is not an easy age in which to live or create. He sees too far ahead to be complacent or comfortable. Unlike the economists and sociologists with their charts and graphs, he knows that the problem isn't inflation or bad housing, but man himself, and that a sharp drop in the price of oil or coffee beans, for all the excitement such a drop would occasion among editors, congressmen, and parliamentarians, would do nothing towards solving the central moral and psychological dilemmas of our time.

There's a huge possibility that the "ism" that will triumph over all the other competing "isms" in the near future will be cannibalism. Will the erudite cannibal want to read Shakespeare or Goethe? I wish I could shout a loud and confident "NO!" But human nature has revealed itself to be infinitely adaptable. Didn't men and women in the heart of Christianized Europe look on silently while six million people were murdered before their eyes, without any falling off in their attendance at operas, concerts, and poetry readings? How many people made any protest when those six million were being led off into the horrendous death camps or were being machine-gunned in the forests? Who? The pope? The German bishops? The Italian, Polish, Roumanian, French, Greek poets and short-story writers? Or maybe the protests came from distinguished film-makers, composers, and muralists?

At this moment, there are slave camps in the Soviet Union and its client states. The prisons in Poland, Roumania, East Germany, Bulgaria, Cuba, Iran, Africa, and South America are overcrowded with dissidents and critics of their infamous regimes.Do the daily beatings, mutilations, and torturings—of which the well-fed citizens in those countries are of course fully aware—in any way interfere with the production of encyclopedias, violin concertos, or novel methods of assaying literary worth? Is the applause for the gifted ballerina or actor any less noisy or enthusiastic? Are the newspaper columns less fulsome in their praise of art and more adamant in their condemnation of atrocity, and are they less eagerly read? Is there any limit to the amount of mendacity and corruption human beings can be conditioned to accept? Personally, I don't think so; their capacity, I long ago concluded, is limitless; their resignation appears so complete and despairing. Culture, never to be confused with Art, is the big lie of our epoch, the lie that makes it easier to swallow all the others.

Still, it's hard, if not impossible, for me to break a habit that it has taken almost half a century to form. Today, only words, artfully shaped out of passion and integrity, have any meaning or validity for me. All other verbiage I regard as excrement on floral bumpaper. I recall saying to a friend, "When my head is soaped by time, I hope I shall have enough craft and wisdom to compose a handful of lyrics that say with concision and intensity what living on this beautiful and dangerous planet has meant." I am immodest enough to believe that such lyrics will be found in the present volume by the alert and sensitive reader, and am sanguine enough to think that such a reader still exists. When women, homosexuals, proles, and blacks are at last free and equal, people will still continue to experience grief and rapture, want sex, grow old, and die. Enduring poetry keeps these constants in mind, whatever the earth-shaking changes in foreign policy and government.

JOHN McAULEY

Concrete Poetry: The Story of a Further Journey

The pictorial foundation of writing can be substantiated by many more anecdotes than I can tell here, but I will relate two which validate this cultural response. In the late 18th century an Englishman was shipwrecked and cast ashore in the Tonga Islands, a kind of paradise. There a white man had never been seen before, and was considered by the native inhabitants as a ghost returned to the land of the living. He began to write a narrative using a solution of glue and gunpowder. The King became very interested in the 'ghost's' activities and commanded that his name be put down in the mystic signs. When the sailor did this the Royal Name was read aloud. The King was greatly bewildered as he gazed at the script which the 'ghost' had scribbled. The King frowned and said, "This is not me, where are my legs?" Further afield from an earlier period, Chinese tradition ascribes the invention of writing to the dragon-faced, four-eyed sage Ts'ang Chien who saw in the stars of heaven, the footprints of birds and the marks on the back of a tortoise, the models for his invention of written characters.

These two versions of the pictorial origin of writing also make known to us the power writing once held, a power of enchantment which has been encircled by and immersed in a sea of print in this Word Age. Now, the concrete poem is a transmutation 'subito pianissimo' of the *pictura* that is speech, expressed in primitive though exalted glyphs. The concrete poem still retains the ancient power of picture writing because it shows, rather than tells, the way a tarot card centers reality.

It seems quite possible that picture writing, concrete poetry and tarot are continually created in the face of a hidden knowledge once truly serviceable to man. This can be inferred by one outstanding actuality: the library of Rameses II at Thebes bore the inscription 'The Hospital of the Soul' over its entrance. But this hidden knowledge was lost, at a later date, in the destruction of the great library at Alexandria in Egypt where a million zephyrous and fragile manuscripts had been centralized from all over the ancient world. The secrets of reality those manuscripts contained we would call occult. It is said they documented the scenery and allurements of the 'Great Time' before the over-civilizing of man.

While tarot has remained in the occult camp and picture writing in the hands of isolated tribal shamans, only concrete poetry (an offshoot of both) interests the contemporary wordsmith because it offers the observant poet an opportunity to work with the *occultation* of experience on *his* terms. For the pictura, concrete poem and tarot, form becomes a limitless source of content beyond the 'forbidden lines' where narrative expression fails to reduplicate the pattern of its intensive parable, its beginning, middle, its moral logic and end. Concrete poetry penetrates words letting space confide its secrets without the slavery of comparison that words can sometimes cause in their urgency to be understood. Consequently, concrete poetry suffers no convenient imposition of rhetoric and maps instead the all clear region of intuition where consciousness and the unconscious meet. A concrete poem is simply a decorative score composed of two salients, with any distinguished continuum known as a 'head band' and any fading area called a 'tail band'.

The beguiling simplicity of a concrete poem should not mislead us into the assumption that it represents mere typographical fiddling. We must remember its origins in the hidden knowledge of ages past. It preserves a persistent connotation that names are integral parts of images and objects, though the modern alphabet of Phoenician invention to expedite trade and commerce has almost lost this attribution. Yet today, concrete poetry continues to revitalize older embodiments of hidden power, transforming the consonant *M* for example, into a nocturnal owl or altering other letters such as *A* from its status as vowel and article into the soaring diurnal eagle, all partners in an endless passage.

JOHN McAULEY

Newspapers and Open Field Poetry

It isn't far from the truth to say that a poem is shaped or designed with the influence of the newspaper lurking at the back of the maker's mind. In a single morning 'The Montreal Gazette' sells more copies in this city than does all the new poetry published across Canada from New Year's Day to Christmas. In one year the people of Montreal read a mind boggling number of newspapers, which if collected and stacked by the Fire Department would create a tower casting a shadow at daybreak from Mount Royal to Los Angeles; a shadow that by noon would cross the icy crest of the North Pole. Time devoted to this wanton consumption of news, symbolized by an albeit improbable sweeping shadow so vast that the continent itself becomes a sundial, shows the scope of people's psychic need for newspapers to interpret and clarify the world and their place in it. Reading newspapers is a popular ritual—as pervasive as brushing teeth. The daily consumption of newspapers indicates the population is hooked on a gargantuan habit. Newspaper strikes are especially hard for people to bear. When denied a major newspaper, they will turn to supermarket tabloids and drugstore scandal sheets just as dope addicts smoke seeds and hash pipe scrapings to avoid going cold turkey. Clearly, newspapers provide a cosmic "rush" in print. If poetry ever had this kind of effect on a population maybe Homer and Virgil knew something about it, but those days are gone. Newspapers have stolen poetry's circulation by casting everyday legends. It appears the public appetite for news has increased exponentially. This is a fair assumption considering unlike the classical notion that heros were to last as long as white marble, a contemporary saviour like Jim Jones becomes a devil overnight having instigated a grape kool-aid crusade into the Hereafter. Public attention may be brief but it is demanding, the public is fascinated by death. Sacrifice seems larger and more real than life.

Perfect for saviours and heros is the newspaper's inverted pyramid style. Its mode is to present the most important fact first—followed by a train of lesser facts. The problem with the inverted pyramid style is that it defies gravity, the pull and tug of reality, causing facts to float in a romantic cloud of history. But why should interpretation of events be subordinated to a set formula or method? Newspapers outlive their founding editors and generations of journalists: all believers in an impersonal journalese. Traditionally, they are members of the Fourth Estate fulfilling the dynamic function of giving the public what it wants, a vicarious high of tragedy, crises and comedy in a patchwork of sheets taken from wire services around the world. Newspapers print for the public good, hence journalists collaborate with society rather than with life. The fatal error of the romantic journalist is that he, like the misguided evangelist, imagines himself to be a measurer of life and finds truth in a hierarchy of facts, the latter in paranoid revelations.

Today, poets are practicing an unheard, unread craft, writing persistently as the last repositories of individual conscience fashioning, in the words of Frank O'Hara, "visual biographical emblems." The poet doesn't glorify the plight of an individual in the manner of a journalist, the poet explores and experiences an event and its consequences simultaneously as he creates, travelling the pathway of art which Geoffrey of Vinsauf wrote about eight centuries ago in 'Poetria Nova'. The poem follows a loose and adaptable periodic pathway and reveals first what was later in time and defers the appearance of what was actually earliest. The poem's path leads to the discovery of a pyramid, apex up, firmly grounded in the sands of life. The periodic structure of poetry is life's imprint in the affirmative language of our hearts and minds, our emotions and desires.

Many years ago a Frenchman, Stephane Mallarmé considered the subtle psychological influence of newspapers in an inscrutable observation;

> It is a virgin space, face to face
> with the lucidity of our matching vision
> divided of itself in solitude, into halves
> of whiteness; and each of these is lawful
> bride at the wedding of the idea.

What Mallarmé was getting at is that the page of a newspaper is a collage-like mosaic of varying typefaces, designed for the eye like Greek temples. Fortunately for poetry, Mallarmé's discovery of the page as a habitus for words remained attractive for others. The Imagists and succeeding poets like Charles Olson all took Mallarmé's brides to ceremonial vows proclaiming an old Arabian proverb: "The eye sleeps until the mind wakes it with a question." The marriage of the newspaper mosiac with the periodic design of the poem has become known as Open Field Poetry. This cohabitation is based on the virtues of form as the key to life. Words in a periodic mosaic express parenthesis without subordination. Words become democratized in a way Whitman never dreamed of.

While the newspaper mosaic locks language into the linear and vertical grid of a chronicle of facts it remains a superficial historical tableau. The poetic mosaic depicts a gathering of voices in isolation, a harmony of self-ironic images and a composition of metaphors crafted by an intelligence spanning nothing more than the poles between inner and outer worlds of possibility. The poet's concern with individuality and subsequent search for individuality in the form offered by Open Field Poetry has given the art its first advance in *Amplification* (the technique of expansion) since the codification of tropes and figures in Classical times. A quotation from 'The Descent' by William Carlos Williams will, I trust, clarify the thrust of this explication.

> No defeat is made up entirely of defeat—since
> the world it opens is always a place
> formerly
> unsuspected. A
> world lost,
> a world unsuspected,
> and no whiteness (lost) is so white as the memory
> of whiteness.

ANNE McLEAN

Notes for a Post-feminist Poetry

1.

For women speech is absurdly problematic. Too much intellect is "unpleasant" in a woman. So the average woman's speech is private speech, tied to the rhythms of day-to-day survival, a notational system for all the details of private lives. Women who use this speech to excess are called "gossips", "busybodies", "nagging wives". But women poets are hampered by loyalty to this time-honoured feminine language as much when they embrace it (in 'housewife' poems) as when they rebel against it (feminism).

The truth may not be what we've been thinking. For women, silence may still be golden—at least some of the time. Much is lost in the transition from private to public speech. Many men grow rudderless without a woman's mute support. Many women don't realize poetry's just another master; a woman who invites it had better know what she's invoking. Beyond speaking-in-tongues, automatic writing, and dream-journals, and well beyond the chronicling of daily life, is poetry. A bit of a monster for all we know. And if you don't like a man knocking you around, why let poetry? Poetry's less interested in you personally. And doesn't even pay *half* the rent.

And after all, maybe the world loves you silent, wants you compliant. A sweet face in a distant corner of the room. Beautiful until you opened your mouth and blue murder poured out. Why disturb the domestic calm, why kill whole trees to publicize speech that only circles the same nothingness which has driven men to sacrifice themselves in work, in war, in art, all these years? Why unearth secrets which might best be kept locked in peaceful, pastoral, womanly bodies?

2.

The lack of a feminine poetic tradition is a handicap for women. The ancient oracles, seers, witches, are our unconscious precursors. These anomalies command little respect in official literary circles. The gifts of the medium may come easily to women, but they can be an obstacle to poetry.

Men make notoriously uncooperative muses. Propitiated, the black-caped incubus is unreliable at the best of times. Dispensed with, he often takes poetry with him. When the macabre vein has drained itself dry, there may be nothing more to feel "intense" about.

Generally, women are most honoured for their purity. Experience is said to pollute them. A female Baudelaire is a whore.

But a whore is a whore, not a poet...though she may be a step in the right direction. As a whore is a woman who has abandoned private sex, so a poet may be a woman who has abandoned private speech. The discipline, the risk, seem similar.

In ancient Greece, prostitutes and poets were traditional companions. Perhaps it's only natural . . .

3.

Strippers and prostitutes practise the oldest feminine art forms. They have a lot to teach women who write. They are good models, first of all, because their degradation is so obvious. None of this wistful devotion to "things of the mind" and no hope of making it on men's terms.

Secondly, they reveal our own tendencies and weaknesses. They embody the woman as Object, totally conscious of herself as object. They remind us that as writers we tend to duplicate that role: we tend to make ourselves the Object of our own writing. WE are the mystery we are unveiling. So is a stripper, taking off her clothes. But she knows that. We forget. Because we forget, we lose track of our own aim in writing, which may be different from men's. And maybe justifiably so.

The stripper appeals to fantasy. Hers is the art of double-entendre. Her act is based on timing: on the tension between what is revealed or not revealed at a given moment. SUSPENSE. We know what's behind the G-string, but we're eager to see it. CON. Is anything really there at all? Is she substance or whirlpool?

As writers we should extrapolate from our bodies to our writing and ask: is anything really there at all?

Humour and self-knowledge are everything, the secret weapon. We should assume the worst aspects of what is said about us. We should learn to write as sub-humans without honour, without substantiality. We should BE that Zero, that gaping hole. It's bloodcurdling to imagine what such creatures would say. What awesome utterances.

If anything, a horrifying puritanism underlies most feminist writing. Women should find the generosity to embrace men's projections. There's some truth in everything negative that has been said about women. Women should not be afraid to explore their own "inferiority". The last thing they should do is blast the world with their denials, or prattle about creating The New Woman. The Old Woman will suffice for a few more centuries.

4.

Sometimes the source of our expression is a desire to heal, to soothe, to explain. Again, we are tied to a tradition which is outside poetry. Speech itself is not what we value, but the emotional content of speech. Women's writing, when undeveloped, can be hypnotic in its effect. Long on connective tissue, short on muscle. Sometimes it's so insubstantial, it's almost self-erasing.

Perhaps it's ourselves we are trying to heal with these lullabyes. Maybe we are trying to heal the rift caused by our assuming the right to public speech. Sometimes we wonder whether we shouldn't have kept our mouths shut and stayed at the creek to pound the clothes. Sometimes we wonder if, by demanding that our private visions be published, we haven't put men in a double bind, got their backs up.

It seems men find it painful to listen to women. Perhaps we're saying the wrong things? Perhaps we're betraying some sacred secrecy? Maybe the next stage is living through the aftermath of our own revolt, as men take revenge for what we have done with our freedom.

5.

So many of us are off our heads anyway. Many will jump in while the current fashion for women's writing continues. Let's face it. Few will float.

Being a woman is an especially lousy reason to write. What does the writing, when good writing comes, is no woman at all.

STEPHEN MORRISSEY

The Insecurity of Art: 5 Statements

1.

a challenge exists in life & art and that is the challenge to be totally free. art can be a part of this challenge, a part of the adventure, & yet we use art as a shelter, or we stifle the creative process with fear & worry and manipulate our work so that it becomes a safe & respectable thing to do. art has been divided from life and we shld attempt to end this division, it is a division which denies art and life. within all of this is the idea that the self is not the center of art; but only by seeing the self clearly can we be free of it, however momentarily, & not thru any amnt of suppression or repression, or so-called meditation. increasingly I am interested in working cooperatively & the traditional ways of being an artist, writing a bk or having a solo show or wotever, really dont hold too much relevance or interest. in our "garden nerns" show at powerhouse gallery pat walsh & I workt cooperatively (as cold mountain productions) mixing & pouring 7,000 lbs of concrete, pouring it into holes dug in the earth, & then moving it to the gallery. we neednt work in isolation when it is possible to join other people in free expression & cooperation. but this can only be done if one is vulnerable & allows the insecurity of life & art to be realized, which partly means seeing that the self with its preconceptions abt wot is art & wot is not art has nothing to do with the work except as a point of departure into the work.

2.

any movement to create an individual style eventually presupposes saying things in a certain preconceived way, having a definite way of seeing reality. style is the self in another form, the self demanding continuity in words and ideas and, eventually subordinating saying anything new to a whole array of ideas & opinions abt who I am & wot I believe, cutting off any perception of the new with presuppositions and the safety of the old. style that becomes consistency in writing becomes conformity to the past; while in fact each piece shld be new, we shld move thru a cluster of styles; style as a transitory event, not as a conclusion which manipulates reality to agree with how one writes. either one moves with the demands of reality or one's work atrophies. if we work according to formulas and rules art eventually gives way to shadows and darkness, to an area of the mind which seeks security in the old and finds only the dulling repetition of the past & the self.

3.

Krishnamurti writes that art is skill in action & differentiates between expression & self expression. a clever mind, a mind cultivated with knowledge and experience, can turn out a reasonable poem, but to investigate something without the center, the center which says there is a right way & a wrong way to see things, that investigation is an art, whether poetry or the art of listening, listening without the center, without thot. or to write a poem which is an expression of a certain quality of the mind, a quality of austerity & humility, of not knowing, of insecurity, which isnt being aware from a position; the expression of this quality of the mind which is sensitive to reality seems to me to be essential to art and life, & not merely the repetition of the past or remaining within the security of ideas and beliefs, where the mind can move only within the field of the known and the dead.

4.

one of the biggest errors is to separate the arts, or to claim someone is more of a visual artist than someone else becuz they have been at it longer. as soon as we bring time into art we are back into the games of society. becuz psychologically freedom is a perception which has nothing to do with time. and unless art is a perception, that is, a moment of free expression, of passive awareness & insight, then we are back into someone being more of an artist than someone else becuz they have been at it longer. art has nothing to do with time. you do it & if it's a "good" piece or not doesnt depend on how many pieces you've done before but on the quality of perception which creates it. as soon as we bring time into art we set up grades and divisions, who is superior and who is inferior. skill to hold a brush or to write a coherent sentence requires chronological time, clock time; seeing things clearly, freedom of perception, psychological freedom, has nothing to do with time or the movement of time as thought. it seems to me that art lies in this perception which radically changes all aspects of one's life.

5.
real art lies in the insecurity of life. as long as we live or create by formulas or promote some ideology or point of view, a set of beliefs or opinions from which we interpret, analyse or speculate abt life, then we continue the past in a modified form. the only creation there is lies in a perception from insecurity, security based on the accumulation of thot, of the past, creates nothing but contradiction and narrows both life and perception. everyday is a new creation but we attempt to meet its challenge with the old. the old brought into the present creates nothing but unhappiness and conflict. the very joy & freedom of art & life is the hidden presence of insecurity.

KEN NORRIS

Some Notes on the Composition of Poetry

1.
What fascinates me most about poetic theory is the fact that no matter how persuasive a theory may be it is never absolute; nor has poetry ever been absolutely defined. Say it is one thing & it springs up as another. It is, undoubtedly, the most resilient literary genre, possibly absolute only in the sense that it is absolutely amorphous; but not really. One has the inner sense that poetry may be approached from an infinity of angles but that the achievement of the "poetic" is a very specific thing. We may approach from many different geographies, take different trails, waterways, tunnels under the earth, jet patterns across the sky, but when we arrive it is to the one & only Fort Poetry. This essentially means that form & content are variable; the one thing that makes a certain kind of writing recognizable as poetry is the "effect" that it has upon us, manifested in the guises of phanopoeia, melopoeia, and logopoeia.

It is the province of all literary art to illuminate the world. How the genres differ is in how they proceed to show us reality. Prose fiction and non-fiction give us a description of the world and society so that we may better come to understand them and their inhabitants. Though the novel may be a "bright book of life" its ultimate goal is secular, originating as it does out of the realm of rhetoric. The way that the short story illuminates is by the process of revelation or "epiphany". It is tinged with mysticism in that, at its climax, it parts the veil to reveal the true nature of reality, incident, character. In its concentration upon fewer characters & a smaller scope of society, the short story cuts deeper than the novel into the territory that it investigates. What we find in drama is the ritualization of human action. The god Dionysus is the prototype for all dramatic tragic heroes who, through the process of ritualization, are elevated and mythicized. If anything, drama reaffirms the patterns of human existence in their purest forms. In tragedy we recognize the truth of our guilty existence and it purges us of pity & fear; in comedy we are often shown the power of human love and of fate as they bring about a happy reconciliation and conclusion.

When we turn to poetry we see that we are dealing with an art form that attempts to illuminate through the process of invocation. Poetry does not so much invoke deities as it does a state of pure consciousness. Poetry is the literary genre that is most inherent to the self; it pushes past the phenomena of event, personality, and thought itself to the very center of being. It is one step beyond drama, in that drama stops at the level of revealing the truth of human existence. Poetry pushes on into the non-human terrain of pure consciousness & pure being. It is the one art form that can take us totally out of the world & give us a taste of heaven, a moment of grace flooded with the splendor of enlightenment.

2.

In its purest state poetry is visionary & oracular. Whether this condition is couched in the language of Layton & Klein, in which they refer to themselves as being in the direct line of the great Hebrew prophets, or in Jack Spicer's notion of "dictation", poetry is something for which the poet is only the medium. The poet is not the creator as much as he is the voice of some force or power that seeks articulation. He is not in control of the language; language is simply the fabric out of which that which must be communicated is cut. The poet may bone up on the language, consciously undertake a study of it and how it works, but all his effort will never make him its master. It is only inspiration itself that can alchemize the language & charge it to the utmost degree.

Here I am talking about the perfect poet, the ideal case. Even the great Hebrew prophets, when they were railing at the gates of Babylon, were throwing in a few touches of their own, some ornamentation here, some rhetoric there. So that the oracle can never be totally pure as long as men are serving as mediums. But whether the oracle is framed by a subjective speaking voice or an objective voice that occasionally throws in a bit of direction and color, one thing is clear: it is the oracle or vision that commands the field, that is to be the focus of our attention. Whether the poet's method is kinetic or meditative, he will be trying to carry our consciousness on into a veritable New World. The dynamism present in the kinetic approach generates a field of energy which, led to its extreme, would blow reality wide open, explode it to reveal what is on the other side of it. The meditative poet tends to bring the world closer and closer to a state of Absolute Zero, where everything we recognize as worldly phenomena stops and another reality can be apprehended. Visionary poetry shows us something that does not exist anywhere in the world of our experience, and there is little place in this new terrain for the self-personality of either the poet or the reader.

3.

If we are to apply a hierarchy to poetic forms, then it is the epic poem that comes into consideration after visionary & oracular poetry. The epic is, by nature, racial or national. It objectively tells the story of an "elevated" enough interest, be it the tale of Odysseus' wanderings as he tries to get home or the building of a trans-Canada railway. By & large the traditional epic is out of place in the twentieth century, E.J. Pratt having been one of its last practitioners. In Pound's *Cantos* & Williams' *Paterson* "the story" is told through layers of history, impression, & experience. The "long poem" still bears some relation to what has been known for thousands of years as "epic". In bpNichol's *the martyrology* we witness a subjective epic of the language itself. The epic impulse has been transmuted until now only vaguely resembling its old guise; in essence, "story" has been sacrificed for an openness of expression. This is the result of a change in voice, the standard of "objectivity" having been nullified in the long poem form. The poet is free to move in & out of voices, states of consciousness (i.e. *Slinger*), in and out of the filing cabinets of fact. Hero, setting, style, action, the presence of supernatural forces are sometimes discernible; more often they are not, in that they are inconsistent (i.e. variable, changing, amorphous). The straight narrative in poetry has, by & large, died a gruesome death.

4.

One phenomenon we have witnessed in the poetry of the 20th century, particularly in Canada, is the fading of the dramatic line of poetry & the rise of a new reinforced poetry of rhetoric. In Canada the influence of Eliot's "Prufrock" is greatly overshadowed by the oratorical meanderings of an Al Purdy or the satirical poetry of an F.R. Scott. I have stated previously that the epic poem is racial or national; rhetorical poetry is to be noted especially for its consciousness of nation, class, political persuasion. A vast majority of Canadian poetry falls into this category, poetry that would persuade us of our national identity and of the strife between economic classes; the historical/documentary poem also falls into this class in that it recreates the sinking of "The Clallam" or the struggle of farmers in PEI against the landlords in the 1800's in order to persuade us to a view. It is in this "form" of poetry that we find the poet most eloquently exercising his public speaking voice. The tone is, by and large, objective; the "facts" are being related to us. However, these facts are couched in a profusion of rhetoric which is providing a commentary *about* the facts, in essence telling us how we're supposed to feel about them. This is a poetry in which the poet is very consciously in control of the language; the poem has an idea or a doctrine behind it and the poet has to make sure that the poem embodies that specific idea. In this kind of poetry we are a long way away from the supernatural oracle of visionary poetry. Poetry of rhetoric is very much rooted in the humanist tradition & has many ties with Neo-Classical English poetry. The apogee of this rhetorical poetry in Canada was the social realist poetry of the forties. It "realistically" depicted elements of the world while, at the same time, interpreting the presented reality. The paradox of realism is that it isn't real at all; it doesn't really communicate the "reality" of life as much as it considers the trappings that are accrued to a certain way of life. In other words, it circumscribes "reality". Often the rhetoric we encounter is an attempt to get at the very truth of the situation (i.e. in presenting a portrait of a worker the poet may try to rhetorically point out to the reader the fact that the worker is being screwed by the capitalist system). To say that poetry is rhetorical is not to necessarily find fault with it; my intention is primarily to point out that this kind of poetry is poet-controlled rather than incarnating a vision that has burst in upon the poet or being a free flowing experience in language.

5.

The most subjective form of the poem is the lyric and it is the one form that is the most abused. Because of its subjective and emotional character the mode of the lyric poem has become the dumping ground for inarticulate self-expression. The novice poet feels that all he/she has to do is to express some intimate personal emotion in order to have written poetry. What is consistently missing is a sense of melody and craftsmanship. At its most subjective extreme, the lyric becomes confessional, fairly amelodic, talky, fragmented, the epoxy of which is the personality of the human being/poet who stands at the centre of the poem. Just as there are only a few real masters of the blues who know how to walk the thin line between blue and self-indulgent, the poets who succeed in the confessional mode are few and far between; quite often they have tempered their obsessions, intellections, neuroticisms with an objectivity that manifests itself in an intelligent working with language. Besides having found an emotional outlet in writing, they have learned how to turn a phrase or to employ a metaphor. At its best, the lyric poem maintains a subjective stance while engaging the powers of imagination and musicality to create a poem that manifests as an instantaneous wholeness. In popular culture the equivalent of the lyric poem is the well-produced, melodic, emotionally evocative three-minute song. It would be misleading to say that the lyric poem steers away from thought; rather, I would say that the poet allows his emotion or mood to generate the poem, to be the flint that sparks the thought found in the poem. & just as the poet's emotion will direct the poem's thought and metaphor, it will also influence the musicality of the poem. If the poet is ecstatic then the cadence of his poem will recreate that state of ecstasy; if saddened the poem will embody a more plaintive music. It is the emotion that is the controlling agent, out of which the poem blossoms. Unlike the rhetorical poem in which the *idea* demands that it be illustrated or denoted by certain images or metaphors, the *emotionality* of the lyric poem demands that it be evoked & connotated by the image, metaphor & music of the poem. Given this, I would maintain that the lyric poem is often a lot less *conscious* than the epic, dramatic or rhetorical poem.

II

1.

It seems to me that poems are composed under one of three conditions or avenues of approach. The first avenue is that of inspiration, pure and simple. In talking of the process of "dictation" Spicer noted that the dictated poem comes through in about one eighth the time it ordinarily takes to compose a poem. At this time the line of communication between the poet & the Martians is open & the poem flows through freely and easily, coming from somewhere other than the consciousness of the poet. The poet's personality or persona has, for the moment, been put on the shelf, and the poem comes pouring out naturally, totally true to its own nature with as few intrusions on the part of the poet as possible. The poem is something that is coming from "outside" the poet; it is not something he is making up, controlling, giving form to. He is only the agent of a greater power. This concept of inspiration incorporates a romantic view of the Muse. The Muse is not the poet's lady love, mother, or dead sister, but an invisible power that is visited upon him and over which he has no control.

The number of poems that I have written out of pure inspiration or dictation I could count on the fingers of one hand. In Spicer's view the serial poem provides a successful mode for dictation, in that its open structure throws off the reasoning faculty of the mind & lets the poem plot its own course. My own experience with serial poems is that they are never truly free of the poet's controlling hand. At some point the poet steps into the poem, thinking he now knows where it's going & so he begins to direct or influence it in its proceedings. Truly inspired and dictated poems are few and far between.

When I talk of inspiration I don't mean that an idea pops into the poet's head, or a first line pops into his head & he then begins to work a poem off of that. The inspired poem is one that flows freely from beginning to end in one take, does not pause to allow the poet to make revisions, is an ongoing process that fulfills itself when it has created, of its own accord, a certain wholeness of intellection or expression. It springs up spontaneously, uses the poet as its agent/carrier/scribe and, when it is done with him, relinquishes its hold upon him, leaving behind no residual traces of its power other than the poem that has been written down on the page.

2.

The second avenue of approach to the writing of a poem is one that I myself use most often: that of attempting to invoke a poem, invoke inspiration. This approach is analagous to Dorothy's experiences in travelling to and from Oz. Starting out on a farm in Kansas she is hurled by a tornado into a world of color where she has her adventures, gradually making her way to Oz. Arriving there, seeing Oz as it is & discovering the nature of its wizard, she clicks the heels of the ruby slippers she has acquired, closes her eyes, chants "There's no place like home" and departs from the world of the imagination back into her world of mundane reality.

Writing to invoke inspiration means starting out from where you are in an attempt to prove that you *can* get there from here. The poet can begin with anything: a description of a just finished dinner, a poetic conceit, a few lines tracing his view of his own emotional development. The important thing is that the beginning of writing starts a *process* which, if successful, will begin to unravel, begin to reveal. Maybe 10 lines into the writing, poetry will suddenly start to happen; the first plateau of inspiration will have been reached. The poem will then begin to write itself, the poet having relinquished the conscious control or state of consciousness that he started out with, giving in now to the greater power of the poem. Williams observed that the poet thinks with the poem; what Williams was telling us was that, in his approach to writing, the poem is not thought out beforehand, then written down, but that as the poem proceeds the poet's mind becomes an active intelligence. The poet now reaches a sphere in which he can undertake a higher level of thought—poetic thought—as opposed to the regimented logic of the self-conscious mind.

Writing in this fashion the poet will observe that the poem will carry on for as long as its power is sustained. At certain times the poet will attempt to intrude upon the proceedings; this may result in the end of the poem, the line of communication having been severed; if the force of the poem is strong the poet's intrusion will exist as only an irrelevant aside which will later have to be edited out.

After a time the poem will expend itself, burn itself out, come to its own end. The poet is rarely conscious of this fact & will usually attempt, now on his own, to struggle on. This usually goes on for about 10 to 20 lines, although occasionally the poet will continue to write for pages, only to find later that what he has written was just a waste of energy. If the poem ends with a strong image the poet will, undoubtedly, attempt to milk that image for all it's worth, developing it well past the dictates of good sense; when he has caricatured or trivialized it he will usually recognize his folly & stop. In any case, what we see is that within the parameters of what the poet has written there is contained a poem; in relation to what has been written it is really a poem within a poem. It is now the poet's duty to extricate it from the morass of dull, tedious writing he has surrounded it with, to prune out his intrusions upon the spirit of the poem's development and, in some cases, to redirect some of his mistaken impulses that began to knock the poem off-beam.

How the poet treats his material after its composition, how he edits it, will obviously shape its final form. What now comes into question is the poet's approach to the process of writing. He must make a decision as to whether or not he wants the process to be evident to the reader of the poem. Much of the writing that is called "Black Mountain" follows the suggestion of Charles Olson, found in his poem "These Days":

> whatever you have to say
> leave the roots on, let them
> dangle
>
> And the dirt
>
> just to make clear
> where they came from

Other poets might choose to forsake the exhibition of the poem's progress in order to present it as a perfect aesthetic object, devoid of the human touch. In either case, the poem has been born out of the process of writing, the poet taking up the pen and writing in an attempt to generate lines of poetic insight by establishing contact with the well-spring of inspiration.

3.

The third approach to the writing of a poem is one in which the poet "knows" what he wants to write about & so exercises conscious control over the language. This is the poetry of the "well-wrought urn" variety. The poet is, at all times, a craftsman who manipulates and shapes his materials. It is the poet who is in control of the poem. In this poetry language is like concrete poured into a mold or clay shaped by a potter's hand. Obviously the skill of the workman here is all important; if the poet knows his craft well the chances are greater that he will create a successful poem.

This third approach is the mainstream tradition of poetical composition. The poet is neither "visionary" nor "medium" but "maker". The Muse he invokes is a recognizable one and the power & responsibility for the poem lies in the poet's own hands. This time honored approach to poetry is traditionally based & traditional minded; it represents the Apollonian impulse towards poetry. Its philosophy is humanistic as opposed to universist, believing in what can be apprehended through reason and what can be made by craft, in contrast to the universist belief (to which I personally adhere) in the total mystery of organic consciousness and the unknown power which may speak through a poet & which is the ultimate Creator.

MARC PLOURDE

On Translating Miron

I remember when I complimented the poet Doug Jones on his translation of *La Marche à l'amour*, he replied that he was pleased to hear that somebody agreed it was a translation. Some critics had seen it more as an original poem by Jones than a translation of Miron. It occurred to me then, in September 1977, that translations of poetry often meet with this criticism and I wondered why. The answer came about a year and a half later when I was in the middle of translating *La Vie agonique*. I found that to produce an English equivalent of Miron's poetic effects, the translator must be inventive and original, and yet this inventiveness can actually damage his translation if he's not careful. Any originality that appears in his work must seem to be an expression of the author's personality and talent, not his own.

That is sometimes an extremely difficult task to accomplish. The translator cannot live in the author's skin, but his work must create the illusion that he does. Gaston Miron's poems are ideal examples of this challenge. To translate them, one has to find words that convincingly render extreme emotions of passionate love, anger, enthusiastic hope, bitterness and despair. Also, moods and emotions sometimes change very quickly in Miron's poetry. The sudden lyrical invocation that comes in the last stanza of "Héritage de la tristesse" may, in translation, sound unnatural and out of place if the translator doesn't understand why the author put it there and why it works in the original text. The translator's inspiration, then is a matter of insight and acting. Miron's love lyrics may or may not have been inspired by love, but the man who translates them is most certainly playing a role and has to be good at it. It is a difficult illusion to create and a situation that has to be handled with subtlety if the translation is going to succeed.

After I'd labored through the first dozen or so drafts of *The Agonized Life*, my translation became *"agonique"* indeed. I'd soon discovered that a literal translation of lines like "Dans l'envol d'un espace baigné d'eaux médiantes", gave results that were mediocre and sometimes impossible to read. In a way, my work became a long "examen de conscience" on how many liberties and what sort of liberties I could take with the text without misrepresenting the author in any way. It was also like a game of chess where one has to accept certain at times considerable loses in order to achieve a victory. I would read a line such as "ah sonnez crevez sonnailles de vos entrailles", and wonder how I could arrive at an English equivalent that conveyed the same meaning, same rhythm, tone of voice and assonance. Also, my end product had to be a poem and not a mere approximation of what was a poem in the other language only. Robert Frost's witty definition of poetry as "what gets lost in the translation", began to annoy me. That was not acceptable, of course. A translation that somehow turns poetry into prose is not a true translation. It's a flop.

When I began translating Gaston Miron's poems I could work on them only sporadically and so I grew aware of the problems involved haphazardly, as they appeared in one poem or another. This was not good for the translations. What I needed was a more profound and comprehensive understanding of Miron's poetry and the network of ideas, influences, views and values behind it. A small Canada Council grant gave me the time to do some research. I began reading the existing translations of Miron (particularly those by Jones, Glassco and Cogswell) carefully in order to appreciate their virtues and failings. I read the author's prose articles (and later translated some of them) as well as interviews that had appeared in periodicals. I telephoned Gaston Miron and he agreed to try to answer any questions I might have about his poems (I didn't mention the number of questions I had in mind for fear of scaring him away). We arranged to meet.

Miron genuinely wished to be helpful and it showed in his answers: they were straightforward and unaffected. Most of my questions were concerned with the explicit meaning and connotations of certain words, lines, images. I wanted to know, for instance, if he had written the first line of "Le siècle de l'hiver " with Mallarmé's "Le vierge, le vivace et le bel aujourd'hui" in mind. He said he hadn't noticed the similarity until the critics had pointed it out; if he wrote that line under Mallarmé's influence, he told me, he was not aware of it. This didn't cancel some sort of "subconscious" influence, but I felt that it was enough to drop *mallarméen* considerations from my translation. "Le gris, l'agacé, le brun, le farouche", with its rapid-fire enumeration, its staccato rhythm and use of adjectives as nouns, still remained a difficult line to translate. After many variations, I finally settled on "Grey, unnerved, brown and savage land".

The addition of "land", which in the French version is implied and not stated, normalizes Miron's use of language by turning his adjectives-as-nouns into simple adjectives. This was a necessary concession in order to avoid confusion. In English, "grey" and "brown" don't work very well as nouns or as the personified *"tu"*("you") Miron addresses in the poem's second line: "tu craques dans la beauté fantôme du froid". What I wanted above all were words that communicated that haunting, intense, nervous feeling evoked in "Les siècles de l'hiver". "Unnerved" *("l'agacé")* was a happy find, and in the second stanza I was able to intensify it by translating "une campagne affolée de désolement" as "fields panicked with loneliness".

From my discussions with Miron I learned something about the background of expressions like "litanies de chats-huants", "l'à-vif", "la rance odeur de métal", and the exact meaning that the poet invested in those words he had coined himself: *"aboli", "agonique", "rapaillé"*,etc. Some of these expressions had interesting origins. For instance, "la rance odeur de métal" was something his teachers, les Frères du Sacré-Coeur, often referred to when he was a young student in the 1940's. Here, "métal" means money. I think that my translation, "the smell of dirty money", conveys the antimaterialist (or antimercantilist) feeling of the thing.

I also learned that a number of Miron's words are borrowed from the rural Québécois idiom. He may alter these words in some way, as with *"rapaillé"*, a participle he derived from the noun *"Rapaillage"* which means something like "recycled straw". Or he may use the words just as they're spoken: *"brunante"* is one example. Notice that he insists on using this word when he refers to the dusk and never uses a more international term like *"crépuscule"*. Miron has also grafted a number of common everyday turns of phrase into his poems: "comme d'accoutumance" (in "Le verre d'eau ou l'inacceptable") for instance, and "par en-haut là-bas" which I translated as "upland back there". Interestingly, "par en-haut là-bas" sounds awkward by itself, but not in Miron's "je suis né ton fils par en-haut là-bas / dans les vieilles montagnes râpées du nord". I believe that what I learned about the original context and connotations of these words and expressions, provided me with the insight I needed to find, or, if necessary, invent English equivalents.

It also made me very aware of the oral quality of Miron's poems and the fact that colloquialisms, word-play ("raboteux rabotés", "charbonneux douloureux"), explicatives ("et la tête bondieu"), interjections ("ô morsure de naissance") and also rhetoric ("Les poètes de ce temps montent la garde du monde"), are *not* appendages to his poetry but part of its basic fabric. These things must be just as ingrained, must sound just as natural, in the translations. It's something I tried hard to achieve. It's not a coincidence that Miron's poems are so effective when spoken before an audience; obviously I wanted my translations to have that same appeal. I asked Miron to record a half dozen of his poems on a cassette tape and he accepted. When I heard his poetry read aloud I began to notice certain things: for instance,how the tone of "Le Damned Canuck" changes dramatically in the last stanza from sadness, fatigue and frustration, to anger and defiance. Such observations helped me find the right rhythm and tone for my translations. Before deciding if a line was good or not, I would first read it aloud several times along with the original in French.

I remember one incident that helped me discover something about Miron's poetry. I asked the poet what he was referring to in "ô solitude de trille blanc dans le mai des bois". My Larousse dictionary's definition of *"trille"* as a musical term, didn't seem to work here. This question appealed to Miron a lot. He is, I found out, an amateur botanist and has a number of books on the flowers, trees and plants that grow in Quebec. He opened a large book and began pointing out various illustrations, one of which showed a small white *"trille"* or trillium. The trillium flower grows singly, just as indicated in the words, "ô solitude de trille blanc". My translation, which originally had *"trille"* as "bird's song", became: "alone as the white trilliums of May woods". It occurred to me, then, what a vast number of flowers, birds, trees and animals populate Miron's poetry. I took a closer look at his terminology. Miron is specific. One seldom finds "un oiseau", "un arbre", "une fleur" in *La Vie agonique*, but rather "le rouge-gorge", "hirondelles", "geai bleu", "fougères", "froment", "peupliers", "cèdres", "bouleaux", "épinettes", "sapins", "claytonies", "tournesols", "chevreuil" and its mate, "chevreuse". He is not only specific in his terminology but specifically Québécois when he calls a deer *"un chevreuil"* instead of *"un cerf"*, the more international term. It's unfortunate, from the translator's point of view, that there exists no similar distinction in our English Canadian culture where "a deer" can only be a "deer".

I then noticed that in certain cases my translations had somehow generalized Miron's terminology. Where he had "le rouge-gorge de la forge", I had "the red bird in the forge". I changed "bird" to "robin" and made suchlike revisions ("tree-tall years", for instance, became "poplar-tall years" in "Legacy of Sorrow") whenever my terminology was not as specific as the author's. In Miron's poetry, specific is often synonymous with Québécois. All of the flora and fauna I referred to earlier are indigenous to Quebec's landscape. It's important, however, that both the general reader and the translator should understand that Gaston Miron doesn't stuff his poems with the trees and flowers of Quebec as though they were artifacts, things to give his work local color, or furniture. The poet does not merely refer to them or describe them. He lives them, identifies with them. "Chevreuils", "rouge-gorge", "froment" are his own feelings and desires alive in the world.

For this reason, it becomes important that certain lines in *La Vie agonique* be translated literally, whether or not it strains the reader's credibility. "Je suis le rouge-gorge de la forge" must be translated as "I am the red robin in the forge" and not "I am like the red robin", or some similar variation. Mistakes of this sort had crept into my translations and they had to be weeded out. In "Pour mon rapatriement", I had originally translated "j'aurai du froment dans les yeux" as "I will see wheatfields". It was as though I had refused to take Miron's word for it when he said he'd have wheatfields in his eyes and forced him instead to say something more acceptable and more conventional. My new insight into his poetry made me aware of what a terrible mistake I'd made. I revised the line to "wheatfields will flourish in my eyes" and resolved to worry more about the art of translation in the future and less about the reader's credibility.

The translation's tendency to become general and abstract was by far the most permeating and insidious problem I had to deal with. It can turn a poet's unique handling of language into something bland and conventional, and it can make a poem, which is the expression of one individual writing in a specific culture, sound as though it were written by some abstract Everyman who comes from everywhere in general and nowhere in particular. The distinctive flavor of the thing disappears then in a number of subtle ways and the poetry, as Robert Frost pointed out, is lost. To counter this tendency I endeavored to read Miron's poetry more closely and thoroughly. My belief is that a translation can only be as good as the translator's understanding of the original text. A superficial reading produces a superficial and mediocre translation. I began noting certain images and stylistic features that recur in Miron's poems and asking myself why they do. Some insights (the stylistic ones especially) were difficult to work into the text while others led to improvements almost immediately. For example, once I understood the significance of hemorrhagic imagery in *La Vie agonique*, it became obvious that my translation of "de la mort des peuples drainés" (in "Monologues") as "the dying of worn out nations", had essentially missed the point: "worn out" fails to render the physical process contained in Miron's *"drainés"*. *"Drainés"* is a term that the reader may easily associate with bleeding (or rather, being bled), and it's the poet's intention that he does. Also, "Monologues de l'aliénation délirante" is a self-consciously populist poem and the word "peoples" (for *"peuples"*) is more applicable here than "nations". I revised the line to, "the dying of peoples drained out".

As the poet's use of physical terms to describe the process of alienation became more apparent to me, I began to see flaws in the English text. "The face of a ruined people" was not the equivalent of "visage de peuple abimé". The line demanded a physical term such as "hollowed": "the face of a hollowed people". Similarly, it became apparent to me then that by translating "dans les vieilles montagnes râpées du nord" as "in the time-worn mountains of the north", I had in fact turned a beautifully descriptive line of poetry into a cliché. I changed this to, "in the old grated mountains of the north", which is a more accurate translation and also better as poetry.

When the problems I encountered were related more to style and language than ideas or imagery, the solutions I applied varied more from one instance to another. For example, while Miron has the knack of indicating loss and void by using the single negative prefix, *"dé-"*, I could not, without producing very bizarre effects, consistently use either "de-" or "un-" or "non-" to translate that prefix in "déréalisation", "déprendre", "défoncé", "découverte", "déphasé", "décentré", "dépoétisé", "déshumanisé", etc. I was faced with a similar problem when I tried to translate puns, assonance and wordplay without disregarding the exact meaning of Miron's words. In some instances I wondered if the mechanics of the English language could allow it. Could the puns on mother and lover contained in "mon Québec ma terre amère ma terre amande", be translated? My rate of success varied. By translating "raboteux rabotés" from "Le Damned Canuck" as "roughened & planed", I had retained the words' essential meaning, their physical nature and opposition to each other, but I'd abandoned the assonance. However, in the same poem, when I translated "ah sonnez crevez sonnailles de vos entrailles" as "O let the bells rattle and bust in your guts", I rendered the line's rhythm and angry defiant tone as well as matching the near-rhymes of "-nez -vez" and "-nailles -trailles" with "-bells -tle" and "bust guts".

Miron's sense of wordplay also allows him to use a typically Québécois method of intensification which consists in repeating the same word twice. Whether I chose to translate this literally or not, depended on if I thought the trick worked in the other language. So, in "La braise et l'humus", I altered "dans les têtes flambées de ma tête" slightly by saying "among the burnt heads in my skull", while, in "Le Québécanthrope", I kept the repetition of *"pauvre"* (from "il fût pauvre comme un pauvre"), by translating the expression as "he was poor as poor can get".

The poet also creates novel effects by using adjectives as nouns, in the first line of "Les siècles de l'hiver", and vice versa, in "Compagnon des Amériques" ("l'aieule prière de nos doigts défaillante"). And in the poem, "Semaines", he writes a line that has a transitive verb but no direct object to complete its meaning: it's "les balcons qui colportent". I discovered that finding the right English equivalent in such instances, isn't just a matter of copying Miron in breaking the rules of grammar, but rather understanding why he does it and the ultimate goal he wishes his poetry to achieve. For Gaston Miron, the poet's business is to turn the spoken language of his people, "les damned Canucks", into poetry. It's essentially a matter of enriching an impoverished speech. Sometimes he will do this by coining new words like *"agonique"* and *"rapaillé"*, or by reworking common turns of phrase, or by creating adjective-nouns. He uses his craft to make the genius of his native speech come out like the grain in wood that has just been planed. In "Le Damned Canuck" he said of his people, "nous sommes . . . raboteux rabotés", and this also applies to the poems he writes.

F.R. SCOTT

Preface to *Poems of French Canada*

These translations from the poetry of French Canada were made by me from time to time as the spirit moved me, mostly between the end of the second World War and the beginning of Quebec's "quiet revolution" in the 1960's. They are not the result of a plan of work, but came rather as a consequence of my widening acquaintance with individual poets and my growing interest in French Canadian literature. I learned much from them, not only about the society in which I was living, but also about the nature of the poetic process itself. There is no better way of finding out how words can be put together to make a poem than by translating poems, and no better window opening upon a country than that which its poets provide.

The period from 1945 to 1965 was one of profound change in Quebec. The old, static social and religious order in the province was at last giving way before the continuous impact of industrialization and mass communications. This radical transformation is least intimated in the work of Garneau but is forseen in many of the other selections, which my own political interests naturally inclined me to make. Hébert's "Manor Life", Giguerè's "Polar Season" and Trottier's "State of Siege" show the revolt of the individual conscience against the old imprisoning concepts, while a new satirical note is heard in Hénault's "The Prodigal Son", Pilon's "The Stranger Hereabouts" and much earlier, in Jean Narrache's "The Philanthropists". How true it is that the poet, as I once heard Pierre Emmanuel say, is like the scout who puts his ear to the ground and feels the hoof-beat of the approaching but still invisible horses.

I have taken this opportunity of making some minor revisions in my earlier versions of the poems, although in this search for the best word or phrase, as I remarked in my *Dialogue sur la traduction* with Anne Hébert, there is no finality. Even of an original poem it has been said that it is never finished, only abandoned, an opinion for which there is much evidence in the worksheets of any poet and in the revisions that may occur in the course of a lifetime. The author of a poem must select the words and images that best express what he wants to say: this is a process akin to translation. Rendering the same poem into another language makes the task more difficult, but it demands the same sensitive imagination and the same verbal skills.

In the past few years there has been a welcome increase in the translation of French Canadian poetry into English. John Glassco's *The Poetry of French Canada in Translation* (1970) made use of 22 translators. Unfortunately there has been little reciprocity in the process: as Guy Sylvestre points out in his *Anthologie de la poésie Québécoise* (7th ed. 1974), there is no counterpart in French to Glassco's excellent anthology. It seems a pity that Quebec poets of the stature of A.J.M. Smith, A.M. Klein, Irving Layton, Leonard Cohen, Ralph Gustafson, Louis Dudek, not to mention leading poets from other provinces of Canada, are not available in French otherwise than as they may be found in the useful but limited pages of the magazine *Ellipse*. Quebec at the moment is so intensely preoccupied with defending itself against a non-French continent, that the literary climate is unreceptive to any "invasions" of English, even the most friendly.

It is indicative of this trend toward a purely provincial view of French culture in Canada that the standard anthology of Sylvestre —himself no provincialist—first published in 1941 under the title *Anthologie de la poésie canadienne d'expression française*, then for five more editions as *Anthologie de la poésie canadienne-française*, has become in its present 7th edition *Anthologie de la poésie Québecoise*. The reference to Canada has been eliminated, though the collection contains five poets who were not born in Quebec. The million French Canadians who live outside Quebec have been cast adrift. It would be ironic if 'le createur, le poète qui donnera au peuple canadien-français son image', who was prophesied, as Glassco reminds us, by St-Denys Garneau, were to come from Manitoba or New Brunswick.

I came late to an awareness of the French part of our poetic history, though I was born and brought up in Quebec City and my father was a poet. It seemed I had to meet the poets before I met their poems. I was exposed for eight years to a subject called "French" in the old Quebec High School, which I attended from 1908 to 1916, taught by a *français-de-France*, as a newcomer from France is called in Quebec, a Frenchman named Boudreau, who drove the irregular verbs into our schoolboy heads by sheer force of repetition. Of conversation we had virtually none, though I was taught to recite a few simple poems, some verses of which remain in my memory to this day. Three years of more advanced study at Bishop's College under a devoted teacher, F.O. Call, also a poet, introduced me to selected French classics such as *Tartarin de Tarascon* and *Cyrano de Bergerac*, and awakened my taste for French literature generally. Indeed, the first poem that ever appeared over my name in Canada (at Oxford I had contributed some light verse to *The Isis*) was a translation of a *Chanson* of Clémont Marot (1596-1644). This appeared under the title "A Song of May and Virtue" in the *McGill Daily Literary Supplement* of March 1925—and was one of the reasons why I met the editor, a certain A.J.M. Smith, and became a member of the group that founded *The McGill Fortnightly Review*.

As a law student at McGill I of course read the great French jurists such as Pothier, Laurent, Capitant, and thus was faced with this monumental manifestation of French culture. I could understand Stendhal reading the Code Napoleon to improve his prose style. One summer to occupy my spare time as a student in a Montreal law office I translated the whole of the *Coûtume de Paris*, the principal source of the Civil Law in Quebec prior to the adoption of her own Civil Code in 1866. The continuity of Quebec's traditions with old France, and through the civil law with ancient Rome, has always seemed to me a fascinating part of our Canadian heritage. The civil law contributes to the identity of Quebec the way the common law contributes to the identity of English Canada. The public law of Quebec, however, including constitutional, administrative and criminal law, in which are to be found most of our fundamental freedoms, is English in origin, and hence biculturalism is woven into Quebec's social fabric whether or not the people are bilingual.

Nevertheless it was possible to go to an English language school in Quebec City seventy years ago and not meet any French Canadian poetry at all. This is perhaps not surprising, since I cannot remember being given any English Canadian poetry either, though here my memory may fail me; only the poetry of England. Nor any Canadian history, still less American poetry or history. At home as a boy I delighted in the animal stories of Charles G.D. Roberts, but did not read his poems. The small English minority to which I belonged in Quebec was highly self-contained, with deep roots in England, though by no means isolated from the francophone society around it. Merely living in the ancient capital, however, with its historic names and monuments, fed a most important part of Canadian history into my daily life, and I was unconsciously introduced to Canadian poetry when my father would recite to us his own poems, many of them inspired by the Laurentian landscape on which I looked out every day from St. Matthew's Rectory, and beside whose streams and lakes my family enjoyed so many picnics and holidays. By contrast, my school fixed firmly in my mind the dates of accession and demise of the Kings and Queens of England, no mean advantage for someone destined later to teach legal history, and to have to give a calendar date to such statutes as the important ones labelled simply 30-31 Victoria, cap. 3 (Imp.), or 4-5 Edward VII, cap. 42 (Can.).[1]

All the Canadian poets who are translated here—except Jean Narrache (Emile Coderre)—I had personally met, and with a number of them I had the privilege of collaborating in the work of translation. Lescarbot, of course, is not a French Canadian but a *français de France*, yet he wrote his remarkable poem at Port Royal, on the Bay of Fundy, during the first settlement there in 1606, two years before the founding of Quebec. The text was sent me by my son Peter Dale Scott who came across it in the Harvard Library Bulletin while doing research at Berkeley. Apart from its intrinsic merit, it fascinated me because it is almost certainly the first poem ever written in North America north of the Spanish frontier, and because it expresses the notion, very prevalent in the history of French Canada, that France has a *mission civilisatrice* in the new world, a duty to

> . . . build the cities, strongholds, settlements,
> To give retreat to pioneers from France
> And bring conversion to this savage nation
> That has no God, no laws and no religion

This justification for conquest does not distinguish the French from other forms of European imperialism, but it reminds us of the motives that lay behind the explorers and settlers who founded New France.

It was not until the Depression years, 1929-1939, that I came to know a large number of French-Canadians, principally through my involvement in public affairs and the work of the CCF Party. My own writing on Quebec questions helped to clarify my thinking, and friendships were facilitated by the growth of an English-Canadian nationalism in that period with the consequent redefinition of Canada's place in the old Empire and new Commonwealth. The concept of a French-Canadian cultural nation became increasingly accepted, though the word "nation" was not yet in common use. Hence the emphasis on "minority rights" in much of my early constitutional writing. How to build a Canada that would allow the two principal cultures to flourish freely became an intellectual and emotional challenge, and in this endeavour literature would obviously play an important role. I heard the voice of the new Quebec in the poets and in such novels as Jean-Charles Harvey's *Les demi-civilisés* and Lemelin's *Au pied de la pente douce* before ever the quiet revolution had arrived.

I met St-Denys Garneau but once, in 1942; he was staying not far from my house in Westmount and came in one afternoon for a talk. I treasure the autographed copy of *Regards et jeux dans l'espace* he left with me, for which in return I gave him the anthology *New Provinces* that A.J.M. Smith and I had recently edited. Because I read his Journal first, it had a more immediate impact on me than his poetry, which I came later to appreciate. His views on Quebec nationalism I fully shared; his aesthetic sensitivity and anguished self-analysis, to which we had no counterpart in English-Canadian literature, touched me deeply. His cousin, Anne Hébert, was a poet I met often and greatly admired; it might be said that my reading and translating of her poetry was the main incentive which led me on to the other Quebec poets. I should also mention as another link with them the French poet Pierre Emmanuel, whom I first met at the Harvard poetry conference in 1950, and who wrote the perceptive *Présentation* to Hébert's *Le Tombeau des Rois* (1953). He stayed at my home on several occasions when he visited Montreal to talk to Quebec poets and to lecture on contemporary poetry to various French-Canadian literary societies.

In the mid-1950's I used to invite to my house small groups of French and English-language poets to meet together informally. Despite the language problem—there were unilinguals on both sides—we had many lively interchanges. I remember Louis Portugais, then editor of *Hexagone* publications, after reading T.S. Eliot's translation of St. Jean Perse's *Anabase*, looking up and saying to me, 'It's very bad'; and Gaston Miron describing to us, as he sat in my tall rocking-chair, how he had virtually started a new movement among the younger French poets in Montreal by inviting to his rooms one evening some seventeen of them whose poems he had noticed in various magazines and newspapers, knowing that most of them had so far been strangers to one another. They left enthused. A new generation of poets was discovering itself, and discovering its role in the pre-revolutionary Quebec.

It was in 1957 that the first of the *Rencontre des poètes Canadiens* took place at the Maison Montmorency, just below Quebec. I was the only anglophone present—a fact which prompted Jean Bruchési, then secretary of the Province, who had financially supported the conference, to greet me with the cheery—and somewhat revealing—salutation, 'Quoi, vous êtes le seul paien ici?' Next year at Morin Heights, near Montreal, the second *Rencontre* included a number of anglophones, among them some, like Jay Macpherson and Douglas Jones, who were residents of Quebec. The discussions and readings were, of course, almost entirely in French, leaving little time for any English contribution; as is usual in contacts and conversations. There were also displays of new slim volumes and *recueils*. Both groups came away more conscious of the obvious fact that, as Sylvestre puts it in the introduction to his latest *Anthologie*, "Il y a deux poésies québecoises: l'anglaise et la française". The *Rencontre* soon in fact became entirely French; the English Quebec poets separately organised their conference at Foster, in the Eastern Townships, in 1963. Out of that came the volume which Louis Dudek suggested should be called "The Saxophones among the Francophones", but which appeared in 1965 under the prosaic title "English Poetry in Quebec".

In 1975 two important volumes of translation were published: John Glassco's *Complete Poems of St-Denys Garneau* and Alan Brown's *The Poems of Anne Hébert*. The English reader may now appreciate the achievement of these two important poets, much of whose prose work is also available in English. Translation is not only an art in itself, it is also an essential ingredient in Canada's political entity. The walls of silence between the two cultural groups, noted so strikingly in Durham's Report of 1838, welcomed and indeed fortified by certain types of out-moded nationalism, are only too resistant even to modern forms of intercommunication. No matter what the political future may hold for this part of North America there will continue to be a need, I feel sure, for translation into English and French of the best work of the two linguistic communities that must continue to live together on the frontier of *les pays d'en haut*.

NOTES

1. The B.N.A. Act, 1867, and the Act of 1905 creating the Province of Saskatchewan.

DAVID SOLWAY

The Flight from Canada

It should be understood first off that the flight from Canada is not a repudiation but in its own elliptical way an act of fidelity or commitment. The sojourn abroad, the annual excursion, the intellectual diaspora—all this must be seen in a 'Canadian context' of a wider significance than is usually ascribed to the term.

There is a strong feeling in a small number of our poets that Canadian verse is on the whole lamentably parochial and insular. 'Canadian content' as a local rallying cry, a political expedience, is a perfectly understandable phenomenon, but in poetry its influence is pretty well pernicious. In a country so young, dispersed and undefined as ours, the search for roots, inevitably, becomes paramount in many fields and disciplines, but not without an element of disingenuousness. What begins to unite us is not so much the search but the recognition that the search is good business. It helps politicians get elected, enables merchants to peddle their wares, provides media and university jobs, and hands over to the poets a ready-made subject on which to exercise their indefeasible narcissism in a pretence of disinterestedness and love. We devote ourselves to the study and rehabilitation of the native peoples, discharging our romantic sensibilities in hymns, elegies and narratives, forms of pastoral nostalgia that, I suspect, are really meant to testify to the aching sensitivity of the poet himself. We regret the subjection of the Eskimo and seek to establish a primordial identity to relieve the profound anxiety of homelessness that afflicts the 'Canadian' imagination. We breathe the vestigial dust of the Prairies and consider that by virtue of a kind of bio-mental osmosis we have managed to assimilate particles of consciousness that relate us to our Indian predecessors. It is ultimately a quest for ancestors that drives and obsesses us. The trouble is that it is too deliberate, too self-conscious and artificial, and can only culminate in a false sense of identity—as if the aboriginal whose dust we gallop over with such quick, receptive imaginations will ever acknowledge us *his* heirs and descendants. There is no continuity of tradition here, no affiliation, merely a superimposition; and the poet who writes as if he were the conscience of the conqueror, the immaculate witness, the distressed apologist, the maker of amends, is proficient in nothing so much as in the art of self-deception. This is not the practice of poetry but the practice of condescension.

Another manifestation of the 'Canadian content' syndrome is that curious amalgam of nature-and-sociological description. I should confess at the outset that I don't consider the descriptive mode as essentially poetic, unless it is elevated to the plane of metaphor and symbol. Perceptive and compassionate renderings of life in one-steeple Saskatchewan villages, or reverent and meticulous depictions of the Rockies, or recordings of one's emotions in the face of natural grandeur or desolation, or anguished accounts of winter, or what have you, have little or nothing to do with poetry, so far as I can see, for they attribute to landscape a latent or inherent adequacy and power while leaving it largely untransformed by imaginative insight. In poetry the merely factual is merely factitious; the inventory of feeling, whether dry and laconic or passionate and exuberant, is merely canonization of self.

With these conditions and circumstances in mind, the centrifugal urgency that a small number of our poets have felt may easily be accounted for. If the 'Canadian' is anything, he is a largely undifferentiated creature, historically in transit, desperate to belong, stridently infatuated with the idea of landscape per se, busy assembling a ramshackle identity from a congeries of dumb, refractory materials, and turning his humility before place and time into a subtle form of self-idolatry. As for the poets they seem on the whole content with inflated reputations at home and massive obscurity abroad. The theses I would stress is that it is precisely the lack of established identity, precisely the rootlessness, the sense of radical alienation, which is our greatest gift and blessing, and that it is the name Noman which will help us escape from the cave of cyclopean insecurity we continue to inhabit. If the poet in this country has one major imperative it is not to write primarily about Canadian themes, to describe, to lament, or to praise the indigenous, but simply to write well, about anything and everything. It is to smash the boundaries of our insularity, to take all place and all time as our province with a kind of Verulamian relish and ambition. Canada, after all, is not Zion. If we have a country its psychic equivalent is distance, the feeling for horizons; and, really, as *poets*, we have more in common with Blake and Spenser than with Lampman and Roberts.

This is not to place an embargo on strictly 'Canadian' writing, but rather to try and stay clear of centripetal passion and inspired jingoism, and to revel instead in our freedom to travel extensively in all the realms of language, thought, feeling, time and place. Such is our proper dimension. There is, of course, nothing to prevent us from returning again and again, but it should be emphasized that one cannot truly settle in Canada unless one has spent considerable time elsewhere, and continues to get out from time to time.

An identity, then, is not to be constructed by intent, nor a national reality by decree. When this becomes the case it leads inescapably to gasconade in politics, messianism in religion, and in literature to a sort of quaint pretentiousness or a sterile ostentation. The insistent focus on the particular does not necessarily ensue in the resonantly universal, but as often as not in a kind of encysted narrowness that writers such as Flaubert or Yeats so relentlessly condemned. The universality we seek as poets may require a speech rooted in the colloquial, but it also needs at the same time a sense of diction and form that connects with the whole tradition of verse, certainly of English verse, from auroral times to the present. It may require a feeling for place, a lively and intimate appreciation of landscape, but also must be qualified and enhanced by the recognition of landscape as intrinsically symbolic, or as an expression of spirit.

Our poets are most truly Canadian not when they are Canadian but when they are eclectic, seeking tributaries from elsewhere to swell the national brook. The Canadian exigency is synthesis. An identity will come of its own in time, a rich and composite identity, hybrid and syncretic, but no less genuine for all that. But we must absolutely drop this Canadian shibboleth that so restricts and oppresses us, this puerile, involuted and autistic pursuit of our mythical identity, and cultivate a healthy indifference to that collective self-consciousness which is at present one of our most distinguishing, if undistinguished characteristics.

RICHARD SOMMER

A Deer on the Road: Poetry and Practice

Just now I've counted up the years I've been practicing more or less formal sitting meditation, t'ai chi ch'uan, and poetry. To think that pursuits so empty of content, in a way, should have occupied me almost daily for such long and continuing periods, often when there were dishes to wash, wood to saw, dogs to walk, classes to teach! But I notice about these thoughts, first, that despite misgivings accumulated over those same years, I think of poetry as being among the 'practices'; and second, that I feel poetry, with the others, to be 'empty'. Both assumptions are questionable, I myself question them, and the questions lead to other questions, about poetics, about mystic knowledge, about art and the practice of a way. And there is an interplay between these two initial assumptions of mine which makes it very hard to talk about them separately.

The idea of a spiritual practice has, in the West until recently, occupied a very separated and even exclusively monastic or priestly position in most people's thinking: the secularization of art and its modern removal from devotional goals means that with the reintroduction of notions of practice from India, Tibet, China, and Japan, ours may be the first generation of artists in some time to feel the need to ask whether art is or can be a practice, and if so, how?

What I have to say about practice is valid insofar as it is first-hand. About the sitting I do, let me say only that it is essentially simple, not full of splendid and dangerous visions or experiences for the most part (though we all have periods of dramatic inner weather) but most centrally a literal *sitting,* awareness concerned with spinal positioning, patterns of muscle tension and relaxation, the actual freedom or constriction of the breath, its configurations and shape. Thoughts come into it, of course, but if released they go out again too. Sitting is sitting, not anything fancier than that, and its mystery entirely extends from this simple actuality. It lets one experience oneself *in fact*, in the absence of complicating and distracting circumstances and the usual rich variety of occasions for us to invent and project the selves we call 'our' selves. The actions involved in the practice of t'ai chi are more complex and almost impossible to talk about briefly, but their implications are similar to those of sitting: there comes a knowledge of the literal *actuality* of body, in a sense a very simple knowledge with infinite implications.

Neither sitting nor t'ai chi are causes of mystic experience and knowledge. It is essential to a practice that it provide a discipline of receptiveness to and awareness of such experience, and that it provide a continuing and stabilizing ground. Spiritual experience may, at least initially, present itself in intense and fleeting visions, and it is the function of practice to translate these compelling moments into longer sequences of personal and mystic development. For these reasons, among others, practices are necessarily highly repetitive, regularly recurrent in one's life. The repetition of the 'same' act means that distracted interest in novelty eventually ebbs away. As with the intonation of a mantra, where the gross features of the repeated vocalisation and hearing of it yield no new information, the ear can attend to progressively subtler and more minute differences, and then to differences in the receiving mind itself. Ceremonial practices, such as tea ceremony, may not recur daily, but the sense of traditional recapitulation, of repeating actions of others in the past, is still implicit. The repeated frames of a practice empty out, as a word repeated many times empties of meaning and reverts to sound, eventually returning attention to the receiving consciousness itself, a "hearing of the hearing."

With all this recurrence, a practice is never quite a habit, because habit becomes after a while unconscious, and a practice always demands some dimension of intense awareness, and is usually purposeless enough, in any practical sense, to make it hard to take for granted. When occasionally a practice becomes boring, as at certain stages it does, it is all the more painfully so because its repetitiveness is so difficult to blot from one's consciousness. Usually, though, in offering the 'same' frame of situation or action over and over again, it opens one up to the discovery that no two frames are ever really the same. What we wake to is that our being is in time, in change. What we experience change with, changes.

Is the practice of poetry like this? In some of its features, clearly it is similar. When Coleridge notes poetry's "perpetual and distinct attention to each part, which an exact correspondent recurrence of accent and sound are calculated to excite," *(Biog. Lit.,* XIV) he could almost be referring to the attention directed into mantric chanting. And any poet who has taken the craft seriously knows how deeply absorbing it can be even when he or she is not actively composing; for the person engaged in it, poetry goes on in some dimension through most of waking consciousness, and into sleep as well.

With respect at least to the actual composition process, however, there are ways in which poetry is not like practice. Writing poetry is too intermittent, as I do it anyway. It is something I feel in the nature of the doing: in thirty years of concern with it, only twice have I written poems daily for any length of time. On both occasions, once for about twenty days, once for two months, I worked poems every morning at full incandescence which emerged substantially complete and requiring little revision, but the accumulated wear and tear of all that ecstasy and turmoil put a term to the process. Also, my sense not only of the daily poems but of the larger shape of the series of them, was to feel the process moving through a beginning, middle, and end. By contrast, formal sitting has no determinate, climactic, aesthetic shape in the same sense. Beginning, middle, and end create expectations, and as poets we play on them in every poem. On the other hand, any extended practice of sitting discourages expectations in pervasive and unrelenting ways, and paradoxically it seems to be just exactly in the mental clearing, the space of mind left open by the withdrawal of expectations (of personal tranquility, of trippy experiences, of preconceived enlightenment) that the truest and clearest consequences of the practice are discovered. Eventually the sitting simply happens, without any particular looking forward or back, without any dramatic event-shape to it, external or internal; when the sitting is finished one simply gets up and enters the next thing to do or be. Not quite so, for me at any rate, with the creative process issuing in a poem, a process always in some sense configured with the poem's shape, climaxing and ending with it. And for me always somehow disrupting; I usually emerge a little, or more than a little, shaken by my participation in the birth of a poem. I may sometimes feel this from meditation, but not inherently. So one may sit every day, I think, but what starts out a poem a day likely becomes a daily set of verses after a while, and if persevered in, mere writing. What happens to the poet is anyone's guess.

So on a certain level, a practice is a practice and the making of a poem is the making of a poem, to nobody's surprise. Or if poetry becomes a practice for someone, it does so as part of the development by which it is possible for a person to live all aspects of life as practice, in which the ongoingness and continuity is of the whole succession of poetic acts, experiences, ruminations. Even then there is room to wonder whether the poems produced this way are really fully-shaped art at all - or something different, diaristic by-products of the development or transformative process of a mind/person opening to connection with the being of things. Yet I for one don't mind the difference, somehow, and I'm pretty much content to write a poem when that's what's happening, and to sit when I find myself on a cushion.

Yet on another level more clearly linked to the wider vision that somehow emerges with, if not from, spiritual practice, poetry is certainly a practice, repetitive, exacting, endless. Every time we enter the making, there is a beginning which is, repeatedly, the beginning of another poem, but which no amount of practice at such beginnings ever quite prepares us for. Over and over again we begin a poem, through the years over and over addressing a continually new, as well as old, problem. Like the repeated frames of sitting, or mantra, poetry never quite becomes habit.

And then there's that curious assumption I caught myself making at the outset, that poetry was "empty of content." There is the half-irony, but only half, in calling practices empty. Empty of new information, variation, what? The cushion can be a mighty lively place sometimes, uncomfortably so. I don't think I've ever experienced sitting the same way twice. So what is there that is empty about practice that is also empty about poetry?

It is partly that they are both relatively empty of immediate practical purpose or direct moral consequence. Poetry takes place, in the general estimation, in a sphere of fiction, of fantasy, of the hypothetical or the pretend, in one or another ways independent of strict questions of truth and falsehood. As Auden says, poetry makes nothing happen. Nothing marketable, anyway.

I recall experiencing in my own body one morning a few years ago a powerful sensation of dying and then of ecstatic release into endless space at the exact moment, corroborated by a phone call ten minutes later, of the death of a relative half the continent away. The experience shook my settled notions of reality, to say the least, but left me with the intense conviction that there was nothing wrong with this death. I wanted, later, to communicate this *knowledge* to the others in my family, but quickly discovered that they couldn't hear or believe what I had to say. Invited to speak a eulogy, in frustration I resorted to a poem. My communication, presented in the context of the poem, became metaphor, and 'beautiful' for at least some of the hearers who told me that they were moved and consoled by it. My thoughts, which I kept to myself, had to do with this kind of emptiness in poetry.

But there is what we might think of as a positive emptiness in poetry, too, an emptiness perhaps reflecting that space of mind, opened up by returning to the same activity, rhythms, sounds, over and over, which is the truly fertile emptiness. Expectations, purposes, intentions, a whole host of directive and manipulative forms of consciousness normally crowd the foreground of one's mind. To encircle and frustrate them with some ceaselessly repetitive event is to open consciousness, to be able to listen (literally and figuratively) to subtler goings-on. And with poetry there is a very special extension of this emptying and silencing that goes on, that has I think always accompanied poetic process, from the primitive beginnings of the craft. What is silenced at the subjective pole of the process are some of the anxious demands of finite personal ego, seeking security and jealous of its territory and identity; to silence these demands is to enable the poet to accept into consciousness a multitude of paradoxical other selves, other visions, other beings. At the objective pole, what the process silences is the need for a world of separate definite facts and reasons; it allows the poet a vision of the world as provisional, hypothetical, comprehensively aesthetic. Between these poles, it offers the power, felt as more extensive than 'empathy,' of imaginative inhabitation, of a going out toward other beings in imagination, living for a time within their being and seeing with their vision. To demand the literal possibility of this is to miss the point. Within poetry's sphere, everything exists 'as if.'

Shaman, mystic, and poet are one in recognizing and using this connection between a condition of egolessness and the power of imaginative inhabitation. Keats, calling it "negative capability," writes to a friend that "A Poet has no Identity—he is continually in for—and filling some other Body...." (27 Oct. 1818) The shamanist identification with an animal or natural feature in order to release that being's characteristic energy within himself, still persists, for example, in names of bodily movements in the t'ai chi practice form: White Crane Cools Its Wings, Snake Creeps Down, Parting the Wild Horse's Mane. Participation in the identity of divinity, ancestor, or teacher is common to religious systems, just as union, whether through devotion or knowledge, seems the universal goal of mystic practice. Self-abnegation giving access to the egoless dimensions of consciousness is usually recognized as essential to that union, to a vision of connectedness of being and wholeness with the world.

The poet's imaginative inhabiting is primitive and perhaps a latent capacity in all. Astonishing energies may be released with the breaking down of the walls of separate identity, or at least of the inessential, acculturated elaborations of it, and both mystic and poet in their ways become, as it were, those energies. In my sitting the Buddha sits, no big deal considering that what we share is our ordinary humanity.

Keats's insight is similar to the experience of poets of many times and peoples, for whom to be a poet is to become a certain kind of nobody who from time to time is 'inspired,' breathed into, taken over, possessed and made an instrument of the muse, the god, the spirit, the idea, the absolute, the original nature, the beloved, the other-than-self however it is thought of and called. This manner of accounting for poetic creation, as the other manifesting within, is encountered almost everywhere poetry is. Evidently that's what poetic creativity feels and has felt like for many poets. For them, the merely separating traits of the 'I' crowd out and fill up the open place of mind in which the poem forms, in a sense of itself. For them, the discipline of poetry has to do with keeping the space open for the poem-event, not just by wise passiveness and skilled verbal response, but by working towards (or recognizing) a kind of absence of personality.

A further consequence of the poet's self-relinquishment shows in a strange quality of poetic language which has always seemed to me necessary to genuine poetry. It is what I must, helplessly, call its silence. The poet is willing to be in uncertainties and mysteries, and in one way or another his work will reflect this, and will go further: it will evoke and celebrate the unarticulated world beyond the reach of language, beyond the reach of human conceptual comprehension and definition. The real poem is ultimately not defining but heuristic, indicating. It moves beyond demonstrations of its own competence in the verbal containment of reality. Its ambiguities, illogicalities, paradoxes, like those of the mystic writers, point beyond its own nature by pointing to the limitations of its own nature, of human words. Teishitsu's haiku, "Well! Well! / was all I could say / of the cherry trees at Yoshino," evokes the elusive wonder that will allow encounter but not possession or control.

Having come this far, can we say that poetry is, or may be, a practice? I think not yet. The poet's negative capability, his or her egolessness, is specific to the situation of poetic creation, and no mechanism I know of guarantees the widening of the poet's egoless union outward from the embrace of the poem, into the equivalent of the mystic's continual living-in-union with the far more recalcitrant world surrounding. Nothing of course guarantees the mystic's attainment (or is it non-attainment?) either, but the crossover is particularly difficult for the artist, even fully possessed of the power of imaginative inhabitation. Not merely because of the seductive controllability of the work's containing sphere, because the artist aware of any medium knows how incomplete control over it must be, even should be; control is in fact often intentionally relinquished, as another direction in which artistic self-abnegation is to be exercised, as a gesture of acknowledgment toward the implicit silence. There is a further reason for the artist's difficulty in making the transition from practice of an art to the practice of a spiritual way. It is that the work (or if not the work, the special activity of art) is demarcated, bounded, set apart, dedicated to a special aesthetic attention. The artist as such is devoted to this separated province or form of action: insofar as the artist remains devoted to art, he or she remains in a divided and ultimately sterile world. If enlightenment makes of person and world "not two," as one of those wonderful Zen wisecracks would have it, the artist must forego full enlightenment. Most of us do, in any case. And perhaps poets are valuable when they speak from the heart of human ambiguity and conflict; it is then, after all, that their listeners can most easily share identity with them, the value of the game.

A curious paradox, that as poets we must enter imaginatively the condition of suffering we might have thought enlightenment would allow us materially to escape. I'm writing this at my farmhouse on the north slope of Pinnacle Mountain in southern Quebec. The road above our house has been full of cars, fluorescent vests, and guns for two days now. Yesterday, in cold November twilight, a lone deer and I stood facing each other on the momentarily deserted gravel. For an instant, before I shouted and waved my arms to scare him back into the woods, the numinal power of this encounter flowed between us. Ever since that moment, the sound of each shot I hear rips through my mind as though through flesh. Except for that one instant of meeting, there would be no nightmare of inhabitation in this, but there would be no magic either. How to preserve, communicate, the energy of such encounters? If we don't write it, it fades away and we partly forget. If we do, in the description something essential is destroyed. Perhaps there is a middle way in poetry, the art of our mixed condition, not to describe at all, really, nor to define, but to gesture with our words toward, without destroying, the deep silence of our enterings into understanding with the other worlds, the other dimensions of our own. In this, poetry is never perfect, but no practice ever is.

CAROLE L. TEN BRINK

How the Eye Conceives the Poem

One way of being a poet is to let the eye develop images which give speech to hidden realities within the natural world and onward into a realm where only consciousness dwells. This perceiving eye is a conglomerate faculty composed of facets from the physical eye, the imaginative eye, the mind and the heart. But this faculty penetrates directly from the eye and senses to the art form.

Blake made the statement, "The eye sees more than the heart knows."[1] This can imply a hierarchy of different kinds of knowing, from the mind, to the heart, and to the eye. The level of heartfelt knowledge is quite easily recognizable, for almost everyone has experienced, in moments of deep emotion, a transitory plunge into the deeper reality of things, and then found himself a short time later, completely unable to state in reasoned language what he knew. The mystics claim this kind of knowledge.

But to go farther still and claim for the eye an even deeper apprehension of reality takes one into an area not so easily recognizable. The perceiving eye, along with our kinesthetic and other senses, can catch glimpses not ordinarily accessible even in great emotion. These glimpses come as a kind of hieroglyphics with intense impact just as vivid dreams do. One does not 'understand' and yet great clarity is experienced. Perhaps emotions and heartfelt knowledge are too closely connected to one's particular experience and personality, and that creates limitation; whereas this visual and kinesthetic sensing of things can be both more primitive and more refined than the nitty-gritty confines of individual experience, and therefore can take us farther.

Blake made an absolute distinction between the physical eye and the imaginative eye, a distinction which was perhaps necessary for the sensibility of his age. Today we can perhaps think in terms of a fusion or at least a dynamism between the two. This conception of the perceiving eye allows for a great dynamism between kinds of 'seeing' which are visual, sensual, kinesthetic and imaginative.

Painting is based on this capacity of the eye to take our sense of the concrete object and fuse it with a visualization of accrued human meanings. The superrealists, like Andrew Wyeth, hone in on the outer world of objects, with such precise, loved detail that the inner significance rises up like a stream. The perceiving eye must never be sloppy, or vague about the natural world. Great attention must be paid to the integrity of objects. Alice Munro holds this belief when she says,

> . . . when I think of the slanting, patched roof and the stovepipe, the house as a marvelous, solid, final thing, I feel that I have somehow betrayed it, putting it into a story to be extracted this way, as a bloodless symbol.[2]

She is protesting that the meaning of a thing resides in its actual concrete existence, and if her words about that house have allowed someone else to see in it only a symbol of death or a tomb, then her sense of what art must do has been destroyed. Wallace Stevens was expressing the same belief when he said "The pears are not seen/as the observer wills."

But the eye can, without betrayal, go in the opposite direction from Wyeth's superrealism and arrive at another sort of perceptual fusion between hidden and apparent realities. Paul Klee, for example, paints only what his 'thinking eye' sees. His painting, 'Landscape of Yellow Birds' shows a landscape of consciousness in images taken from nature. Each natural image has become part of a genuine language to communicate what his daring consciousness has seen. Klee says in his "Creative Credo,"

> Art does not reproduce the visible, rather it makes visible. Formerly we used to represent things visible on earth . . . Today we reveal the reality that is behind visible things, thus expressing the belief that the visible world is merely an isolated case in relation to the universe, and that there are many more, other latent realities.[3]

The perceiving eye sees in the extremely particular and especially in apparently trivial events and objects shapes of the hidden.

For Blake, nature and imagination became one, when he was in a state of lucid perception. Blake says in a letter,

> I know that this world is a world of imagination and vision. I see everything I paint . . . You certainly mistake when you say that visions of fancy are not to be found in this world.[4]

The natural world becomes a visible expression for the imagination. If, as Fenollosa said, 'The cherry tree is all it does', then its acts of rooting, budding and turning sunlight into green leaves and cherries are profound evidence of imagination in nature. When the artist's imagination taps the imagination of the cherry tree, then nature and art intermingle and reality can be transformed and clarified.

Images used by the painter reveal deeper realities through visual aspects of form, line and color. The poet is one who has the ability to directly translate potent, visual images into their spoken form. The poet gives language to the eye. Thus, through language, the eye is put back in touch with mind and heart, so that the powerful truth of the image can be momentarily glimpsed with fuller comprehension. Only poetry and drama, of all the art forms, can do this. But both drama and poetry have at times become too severely concerned with surface realism.

Now and for the future, artists and poets must go even farther than Klee said they should. Art must not only reveal the reality behind visible things, it must also push and further that reality. In articulating what is not visible, the protean and diffuse in the universe is made manifest and solid. Expanded territories of reality and consciousness are staked out. As the pressure of surface reality intensifies through technology and mass media, so does the pressure of the true poet's imagination intensify in opposition and fling itself full force into the latent realities within consciousness and within the universe.

The energy of the perceiving eye is a tool carving evolution in the sense that the poet's creativity is continuous with the creative force of the universe. The poet's language is a living organism at the tip of the evolutionary process. Poetry not only articulates our most sublime sensibility, it continuously carves that sensibility out of material possibility. Concentration and density of matter lead to mentation. Mentation leads to language which leaps upward to the sky. As Lewis Thomas says in *The Lives Of The Cell*, language itself gives us energy to further inner space, our senseate spirituality.[5]

Teilhard de Chardin expresses a similar idea when he says that human life was first a product of evolution, and then as consciousness perceives more and more how the universe has evolved, it becomes an active force shaping the future.

> Then consciousness as it grows will know and then become everything else. Imagination will replace object. Inner life will be everything.[6]

Or as Blake would say, the eye opens a center in the prison of consciousness; cleared perception turns the eye inside out into the universe.

Poets who dare to take this leap into expanded consciousness need to understand very clearly how word-images work in the human consciousness. T.E. Hulme stated it very well at the beginning of the Imagist movement, when he said that thought is prior to language and consists of images. A combination of images forms a "visual Chord" in the mind. In the effort to communicate thought there must be a direct "Passage from the Eye to the Voice." This is a process of forming sounds which genuinely articulate the image. The result is a speakable word-image, the building block of all verbal communication and of poetry.[7]

Poetry is the forward looking force of language catching these images from the consciousness in their vital and genuine form. Poetry is the sublime capture of our concrete, senseate experience in the universe. The rest of language is abstract encounters.

What can be inferred from Hulme is that poetry must be visual and concrete in the same way that dreams must be, in order to communicate human intuitive glimpses at the unseen. The short life or dead end of the Imagist movement is partly related to the fact that the canon of Imagist principles for writing poetry, if taken literally, really only avoid vague romanticism in order to fall flat on surface realism. But the best of the Imagists, like William Carlos Williams, prevailed, as true poets do in any school, by saying "so much depends," when he talked about "a red wheel barrow" and the "white chickens." Others, like Wallace Stevens, escape the pressure of surface realism all together by saying "things as they are/are changed upon the blue guitar." Yet Stevens never let go of his desire to know "the thing itself, not ideas about a thing." The apparent contradiction in his stance becomes meaningless when we realize that the thing to know is never purely outside or inside. Perceiver object relation is forever dynamic.

To develop the perceiving eye, what must a poet do? First, a poet must look, attentively, with all senses open, at objects in the natural world which forcibly strike the consciousness. This prolonged gaze may produce in the consciousness that Wyeth-like heightened awareness of things in the world. Or long gazing may produce such an upsurge and expansion of consciousness that the thing in the world becomes a vital word-image to express a new found state of consciousness.

Theodore Roethke believed in long looking as a method of achieving heightened consciousness. He discusses it this way:

> It is paradoxical that a very sharp sense of the being, the identity of some other being—and in some instances, even an inanimate thing—brings a corresponding heightening and awareness of one's own self, and, even more mysteriously, in some instances, a feeling of the oneness of the universe. Both feelings are not always present, I'm aware, but either can be an occasion for gratitude. And both can be induced. The first simply by intensity on the seeing. To look at a thing so long that you are a part of it and it is a part of you—Rilke gazing at his tiger for eight hours, for instance. If you can effect this, then you are by way of getting somewhere: knowing you will break from self involvement from I to Otherwise, or maybe even to Thee.[8]

At other times Roethke admits that contemplating objects has the opposite effect; then the real result is a great sense of isolation and singularity of the consciousness and a sense of the totally alien nature of the material world.

Prolonged training in this method of long looking will lead the poet into an entirely unexpected and sinister seduction. A radical alteration of consciousness occurs whereby a wound is opened in surface reality. Objects and events, time and space no longer appear in their conventional niches. Daily experience now occurs as spurts of real perception bursting out of the whale, and interspersed with long pauses while the whale goes down under and the surface events muddle flatly onward. It is as if a deep river of protean realities has been tapped and the consciousness now hungers only for this reality. Emily Dickinson mastered this seduction into a deeper level of reality and writes of it, in one poem, this way.

> I had been hungry, all the Years—
> My Noon had Come—to dine—
> I trembling drew the Table near—
> And touched the Curious Wine—
>
> 'Twas this on Tables I had seen—
> When turning, hungry, Home
> I looked in Windows, for the Wealth
> I could not hope—for Mine—
>
> I did not know the ample Bread—
> 'Twas so unlike the Crumb
> The Birds and I, had often shared
> In Nature's—Dining Room—
>
> The Plenty hurt me—'twas so new—
> Myself felt ill—and odd—
> As Berry—of a Mountain Bush—
> Transplanted—to the Road—
>
> Nor was I hungry—so I found
> That Hunger was a way
> Of Persons outside Windows—
> That Entering—Takes away—[9]

Dickinson is making clear that this hunger is not satisfied from nature, that the entering takes her somewhere else. Once this entering into a deeper reality occurs, the surface continues to dazzle and entertain and occupy one much like a movie which is almost convincing. The poet then is repeatedly seized with the desire to create actual whole experience out of the bits of events which whirl around her and demand fruition. From then on the consciousness is constantly in pursuit. The eye finds word-images which make language into a sword.

Once that transformation has happened, the perceiving eye is much freer to see into things and the consciousness is tremendously released from the bounds of conventional patterns of thought. Thus, a journey of perception begins, for the poet must now find a language that will sustain and chart her way out, as well as report back her discoveries. The language and the perceptual journey become inseparable. Without Hulme's 'visual chord' and word-images the consciousness cannot lead itself along. Without articulation the journey stops, the stepping stones disappear, blackness descends. Also, only articulation assures the poet that her journey is not completely mad but has a communicable human meaning.

The first forays are likely to be joyous, uplifting, and the language required is not yet too difficult. But complications soon occur. This cosmic journey takes place within the context of personalities, everyday events, and nature's parade of seasons. Sexual love and the poet's tie to nature are two aspects which are at times seen to have cosmic dimensions, but at other times they seem totally disillusioning and even become adversaries. Trade offs and compromises and momentary harmonies are created between the personal and the cosmic.

The continuing tensions create deep veins of new perception which are able to move the poet's consciousness forward and back from primordial beginnings to elevated insights. A point of ecstasy is momentarily reached in which the poet's eye takes on power and wields the world in its fist of song. Blake speaks of being "drunk with intellectual vision," Emily says "I taste a liquor never brewed," Roethke sings, "I could watch! I could watch! / I saw the separateness of all things! / My heart lifted up with the great grasses."

Just at this point of realization and visual grasp a slight hesitancy, or intoxication, or unwieldiness makes the poet look back, and like Orpheus, she loses everything. Complete panic and darkness descend. The vision skids away, swerves out of sight and one is left with mere sing-song in the pitch black. This can be likened to the mystics' experience in contemplation. They speak of intense ecstasy and light being suddenly withdrawn and one is plunged into unfathomable darkness. Such chaotic intervals of Dark Night may last months or years before the consciousness again unifies itself around a new center.

Building on that melancholic stone becomes the poet's true vocation. Out of it comes the conviction and courage to absolutely sing, and one begins the spiral journey of deepened perception all over again.

NOTES

1. William Blake, "Visions of the Daughters of Albion," *The Illuminated Blake*, annotated by David Erdman, (Garden City: Anchor Press, 1974), p. 127.
2. In John Metcalf, ed., *The Narrative Voice*, (Toronto: McGraw-Hill Ryerson Limited, 1972), p. 181.
3. Will Grohman, *Paul Klee*, (New York: Harry No. Abrams, Inc.), p. 21.
4. In Evelyn Underhill, *Mysticism*, (New York: Meridan Books, 1955), p. 259.
5. Lewis Thomas, *The Lives of a Cell*, (Toronto: Bantam Books Inc., 1974), p. 156.
6. Teilhard de Chardin, *The Phenomenon of Man*, (New York: Harper Torchbooks, 1959), p. 165.
7. In William Pratt, *The Imagist Poem*, (New York: E.P. Dutton & Co., Inc., 1963), p. 27-28.
8. Theodore Roethke, *On the Poet and His Craft: Selected Prose*, ed. Ralph B. Mills, Jr., (Seattle: University of Washington Press, 1965), p. 25.
9. Emily Dickinson, *Final Harvest*, selection by Thomas H. Johnson, (Boston: Little, Brown and Company, 1961), p. 147.

PETER VAN TOORN

Kosher Carp on the Nuclear Harp

There is no shock in the acknowledgement: poets have chucked their fountain pens. Gone the goose quill which once gave them wings on paper. Business, with its premium on efficiency and rapid response, has accelerated the conversion from pen to typewriter, which the switch from letter writing to phoning started. And the ball-point, the typist's standby, helpful as it is, with its buttery motion, rapid, ready, uniform—ink on wheels—does not assist the cultivation of a sculptured calligraphy. Nor does it serve as a reminder of the symbolic and sacred purpose of the word, its creative reaching for the Logos, the divine word incarnate. A disposable ball point poetics may fail to remind us of the symbolic resonance and dramatic intensity of the poet's ultimate theme—Man—invoked by the vocal plasticity of words, for that is what the shape in the sound of words invokes: the image of man going in and out of sync with his feelings of the divine. The poet taking down the poem with a noiselessly rolling ball point can feel consoled to have this emblem of his Nuclear Muse in her plastic tubeskirt and chrome headgear handy: he doesn't have to listen to the cat'sclaw scratching of a sharp steel nib, or be at the mercy of a pencil going blunt. But he has himself to blame for the laxity of his results, especially if he confuses the blue lipstick on the page with the supreme beauty of purpose hallowed by words, and is counting on the printer's craft for a cosmetic remedy of this hiatus in his poetics. The same observation obtains for all mechanical devices used in writing. But it applies particularly to the typewriter, a standard piece of equipment in the Nuclear Age, providing a system of public address which (like the microphone in the concert hall) is sometimes confused with afflatus.

Borrowing the models for its parts from various mechanical devices, the typewriter accommodates the inventive pulse of the Renaissance, the technical ingenuity of applied science, the momentum of Protestant capitalism, the industrializing aspiration of modern democracy, and the grid pattern of graph paper: it provides every writing oriented body with a mechanical device capable of fabricating a compact, legible, orthographically uniform, marginally squared, and rapidly assembled piece of linear information with the instant glamour of the printed page. It is the market's idol, the businessman's decoy, and the poet's altar piece. Useful as it is, the typewriter has as little to do with inspiration and poetics as the woodpecker's sweet peckery blab has to do with the maintenance of that most modern of trees, the telephone pole. The conversion, however, from pen to typewriter, as incidental to the art of writing as the earlier conversion from dip quill to fountain-barrelled stylus, has curiously enough attracted serious attention because it has reasserted, in visual report, a cherished affinity between poetry and music. But it seems to have made some poets a little goofy in their poetics.

Most of poets of the Nuclear Age, maybe on a tip from Pound's *Cantos* or Olson's brilliant but demagogically inflated essay on projective verse, seem to organize their poetry on, or derive their poetics from, a model abstracted from the utilitarian features of the writing machine. The impulse reflects generosity and trust. Instead of merely typing poems out to present them more neatly, compactly, and legibly, whether to anticipate the typography of the printed page, to facilitate the editor's reading, or to entice the publisher's interest, many contemporary poets regard the structural conveniences of the typewriter's keyboard as essential to the making of poetry—to its 'composition by field'. Stretching certain imagist and free verse leads a little, they incorporate the mechanical operations of the typewriter into the composition of poetry by a sequence of logic that is difficult to follow. The result of their experiment, and by now the coteries are doctrinaire about it, has been a wholesale replacement of traditional poetics by an idiosyncratic typewriter poetics. The experiment has enjoyed a few successful results: poetry of the Nuclear Age is abundant, varied, and sometimes intensely moving. But the successes number among the exceptions, and do not necessarily prove the basis for a novel theoretic model of poetics. When projective verse claims that the typewriter is more than a device for conveniently transcribing 'visions and revisions,' it becomes an experiment that has all the promise of a new art form—all the promise that painting with an electric toothbrush has. The projective aspiration does convey an element of risk: it emphasizes a fresh approach to revelation, by showing an irreverence for technique and erudition, and a reverence for vision. But when it vies with commercial advertising and exploits shortsighted aims and means, it embraces a very ephemeral vogue promising the excitement of getting a shampoo and squeeky hairdo by going in an open convertible through an automatic car wash.

The first thing to strike the reader about poetry composed in the Nuclear Age is that some of it, for all its insistence on everyday experience,on the wide open spaces of continents, free of rules and crowding, rich, without denigrating past, uses more space on the page: up to three hundred per cent, by traditional standards. The desire for elbow room reflects North American desires. A loose easygoing attitude is a feature of the cowboy's rambling life: frontier consciousness is imbued with a general expansiveness. This proclivity to sprawling is reflected in *The Wasteland, The Cantos, Paterson, Howl,* and other poems striving for epic dimensions. The generous use of space, which affects even brief lyrics of the Nuclear Age, may not represent an inevitable direction for poetry, for poetry is not a visual medium. The second impression, decussating the first, concerns the idiosyncratic use of space itself, to wrench functions from it which have traditionally been represented by other means. Lines begin at the margin as soon as any part of the page. Words are present in level rows, but not in sequence. They begin and step at arbitrary depressions set by tabulator or butt of some preceding line with which it has no syntactic or musical relation, an arrangement which seems to be visually enforced, and rigidly as a rule. Some of the margin settings have nothing to do with stanzaic, metric, or thematic organization. The same arbitrariness is true for the vertical tally of space. We want to feel as if we're walking from a girder held by a swinging crane onto a new jumbo construction in middle sky, but our jumping off point coincides with no recognizeable use of versification, intonation, or punctuation. If space represents visually what silence does acoustically—a spiritual continuum—it cannot measure or represent conventions of sound and imagery without the recognizeable use of conventions: indicate a caesura, a modulation in dramatic pitch or pace, a syntactic reflex, and all the cues which the reader requires for interpreting rhythm, tone, and meaning.

The third impression which poetry affecting some notion of projective verse gives involves a denial too: the absence of a metrical continuum or unified rhythmic pattern, with or without rhyme and stanzaic organization. Images are arranged in a visual pattern whose organization, in poetic terms, defies analysis but resembles the contemporary utility style of assembling lecture notes and administrative directives. The collage of perceptions in noteform indicates a recrudescence of the lay-out patterns of advertising and newspaper reporting, and of the conventions of discontinuous coverage used by other media. Projective verse replaces the tissue of connectedness supplied by metric movement and measure, by rhyme, unity of tone, diction, and syntactic organization, with a graphic legend. This legend or spatial license is allusively animated by random statement guaranteed poetic validity by the trademark of an identifiable personality. The noteform format of Nuclear poetry devolves from the use of the typewriter in assembling poetic effusion, without reference to traditional poetics or the technical demands which extemporizing necessitates; it assigns a pragmatic, instead of thaumaturgic, role to words, accepting language as a material fabric, but without a supernatural source of direction for its dreamlike being. Much Nuclear verse posits prosaic limits to verbal efficacy, and makes poetry serve confessional purposes by managing words as if evolved from a visual, perceptual, and practical (rather than from an aural, symbolic, and meditative) order. Given the itch of the concrete poet, the maker of projective verse (and sometimes the maker of stochastic and stichic verse) utilizes the conveniences of the typewriter—tabulators, space bar, variable margin setter, and adjustable platen and line spacer, shift lock, ampersand, slash, per cent, number, italic, and other features of the keyboard—to represent elements of rhyme, rhythm, syntax, punctuation, and logic.

The effect of this kind of orthographic witticism, cultivated by Pound, Cummings, Olson, Williams, and some of the Beats, has been to make poetry look as different from prose as possible. Rewrite one of these poems in less eccentric form, and there are frequently surprises: when the clowning with the typewriter on the page, with its mechanical conventions, is not organically part of the intended effect, not part of a specifically visual design (as in concrete poetry), the rudiments of rhythmic prose are missing. Sometimes what remains is cloyingly sentimental or undigestibly abstract. The overlay of unconventional spelling and punctuation, the distortions or lapses in grammar, logic, and style, and the bare accommodations for unity of tone, rhythm, diction, and image, all act as kind of distraction and irritation. Sometimes these idiosyncracies provide a cosmetic application to a homely theme; sometimes despite iconoclasm, they betray a prosaic flatness. Even some of the best Cantos of Pound are regrettably marred by a self-conscious attempt at making the exotic and sublime readily available. It has the aura of vaudeville about it, but soon stiffens into a grave habit that promises its own demise.

The fourth impression which Nuclear poetry seems to present is one of imbalance between inner and outer, a rootlessness. Even serious work tends to seek a global parentage. Without providing bridges for artistic assimilation, it arrogates modes of other cultures. Curiosity and cultivation in foreign literature and art represent a genuine flowering of the democratic spirit. But one cannot be too strident about material not digested. Pontificating from a culturally elevated and exotic pulpit is difficult to warm to. Frost serves as a better example here than Pound, Eliot, Olson, and others because his allusions to people, places, facts, and events with which he expects the reader to be on familiar terms are not recondite. His poetry shows no residue of his learning. There is a lot of modesty in Eliot's poetry and prose, and much intellectual daring in Pound's, and great beauty in both, but in Frost it sometimes seems more natural. Perhaps this is because Frost does not try to insist on values beyond those appropriate to poetry; he is not trying to save or convert: Frost has neither the evangelism for traditional culture nor the desire to infuse poetry with wide-reaching erudition, which Pound and Eliot do. Frost's poetry may be narrower for it, but it is also healthier for it—his poems are less like museums.

Nuclear poets writing in 'open' or projective verse are after something genuine—no doubt about that. Their experiments sometimes show far more vitality and willingness to undertake risk, to assimilate experience in a lifegiving manner, than the productions in traditional forms by more conservative contemporaries indicate. It may be that, given the image of their poetics, with its technique of expression rooted in a visual basis, the McCoy they're after resists finding out. Nevertheless, their clowning with the typewriter shows a desire to emulate the properties of oriental languages, whose concreteness of representation is vouched for by parallel sources in nature—a specificity Pound insists on when he quotes his Chinese student's definition of poetry as the art consisting of 'gists and piths'. The Nuclear poet's axing of traditional poetics evinces a search for spontaneity and authenticity, for an uneven field, and if not indefinitely open, a grass lot rather than an asphalt court: something with an eccentric surface to play ball on. His more deliberate experiments reflect his aspiration to register the busy, dissonant, demotic, life-imperilled Nuclear consciousness, regulated not by rhyme, metre and syntax (what Pound calls 'the beat of the metronome') but by respiratory system, the measures and cadences made by breathing from the plexus. His utterance is often involuntarily informed by the ancient Biblical and Homeric imperative of catalogue or enumeration; exact or incremental repetition; variability of line length and metric pulse; enjambment or syncopation; mixed or ungraded diction attempting to close the gap between street and academy; colloquial allusions to contemporary events, persons, publications; plastic elaboration of phrase (through use of space); extensive lower case; and absence of graphic punctuation.

The overall impression which the Nuclear poet gives of himself in his poetic method is that of a creator who is disenfranchised by academy and public, and who cherishes disorder, particularly intellectual disorder, as a warning against encroaching slickness. He breaks off, after the fashion of the Beats, in mid-speech, philosophically interrupting himself to 'blow off' or dismiss his creative act. Many of his poems are about the creative act: the word 'poem' or 'poet' is legion in his works and suggests his uneasiness in the bardic role. He places traffic cables over the habits of his domestic life to gather statistics for his poetic imagery. When his cable is 'live' and dangles dangerously over the abyss, his model for creativity is the irrational, electric, surreal area of consciousness. During his oral delivery in public, he supplies some of the ghosts that haunt his poetics—the elements of meter and punctuation, for example—by a swinging of his arms or liturgical looping of his voice reminiscent of Pound's priestly recordings. In his disenchantment with traditional poetics, he displays a revulsion for history and established values in politics, religion, sex, and aesthetics. He disavows any allegiance with the 'dead' poets whom his formal education has given him access to; his pantheon is buzzing with living poets with radical views. He tries to duplicate the syncopative rhythms of jazz and ethnic music generally by staggering his lines and injecting slang and colloquial references to ultra-nonplus nowness. He releases his phrases and chops up his prose fabric as if to acknowledge the outrage of omission and commission, and to remind us of the perpetual threat of holocaust.

Whatever his motives, the follower of Pound, Olson, Cummings, Williams, and more recently, the Beats, Ginsberg, and the Black Mountain incumbents, has turned up with an exaggerated and idiosyncratic enforcement of a poetics which has not always resulted in the exploration of a new range of emotion, the explosion of original thought, the discovery of more condensed and dynamic forms of dramatic rapport, or the creation of a resonant rhythmic idiom informed by twenty-twenty spiritual vision. A poem does not acquire intensity or succinctness because it omits a part of speech or connecting phrase and represents it by a slash, series of dots, or swerve on the page; a graphic rupture, an arbitrary horizontal or vertical jump on the page, does not signify a leap of intuition, measure a change in pitch, count for a pause, cue in a new dramatic voice, highlight delicacy of image or diction, or accommodate variations in rhythmic contraction and expansion; a word does not acquire texture or affect the rhetorical status of contingent words because it is abbreviated or spelled quasiphonetically; the arbitrary violation of the margin does not initiate a caesura, a different tempo, a fresh strophe or tone; the extensive use of upper case or italics does not rivet the reader's attention; similarly, the extensive use of lower case, together with the ditching of standard punctuation, does not celebrate the advent of a saner political order, the location of a discreet persona, the adherence to a credo of spontaneity, the entry of simplicity, or the installation of an unorthodox, typographically achieved poetics; the ousting of rhyme, meter, fixed form, and the full range of syntax, and their replacement by fragments of hypnotic chanting and snapshots of surrealist image orgies, does not promise anything but the undigested disgorgement of inventory from diaries and dreams; the disclosure of phrases from foreign tongues and recondite sources, and allusions to pet concerns (composed of poets, notions of poetry, personal history) do not create a poetic mask or signal the achievement of an integrated vision; nor does the manipulation of tabloid sensationalism advertise anything but the artless. In short, the collage of quotidian events assembled in noteform does not constitute a poetic vision in a metric continuum.

Still, the typewriter can be a wonderful machine to compose on. It will give the lean poet strong arms and a blacksmith accuracy when the poem is hot; it will give his dishevelled garret something of the business air of the age and provide him with the ink, hammers, and bells that, along with his pensive fool'scap, are the accoutrements of his vocation. And though the Muse will visit him naked as easily as in overalls, she favours those prepared for her. Let the poet, therefore, keep pen and pencil handy so he will not be caught off guard if she enters through his skylight without knocking and sits catlike on his typewriter. His pen's onionsharp ink odour will please her, so will the smell and sight of woodshavings curling off his pencil like butterflies. After all, if 'It takes a hero to improve on his father,' as Homer jokes it does in his reference to tradition, the least the poet can do about the Philoctetean dilemma he inherits is to remember that he is a member of a rare species, a kind of self-begetting wife.

PETER VAN TOORN

A Goose in the Caboose

Take away the haiku, and the sonnet is the heartwrencher of all the fixed forms: by opening and closing the heart a little more generously than the compactness of its gesture would seem to allow, the sonnet lifts a burden. So when the occasion it aspires to accommodate is the same as for song and dance—the celebration of thought mastered out of doubt by feeling, in singing words, and in the nick of time—the sonnet is a bouquet of pictures in sound: its syllables touch the heart with a freeing motion. With a 'sweet wild twist' it shows the glow of feelings redounding to the soul, joining a moment's joy and sorrow to sacred waves of being. But before it lifts a burden, resolves a tension, or makes a revelation, before it makes naked the harmony concealed in the very reality to occasion the burden of its theme and energy of its song, the sonnet finds its reason in rhyme, in a tuning suitable to its moody straights. It does this mysteriously, like water stampeding through the bottleneck of a river narrows or talking in bubbles along a slope of stones, quickening from its prosaic stance of doubt into a deeper, more fluently melodious and alive design. The sonnet, like the pine and the pagoda, shows signs of longevity; it is nearly seven hundred years old now. Yet it is always in danger of becoming obsolete unless it remembers to deliberate the contemporaneity of its ancestry, by attending to the revolutions in diction and the rhythms of common speech. So one of the sonnet's themes will always be speech, passionate, musical, rhabdomantic speech itself—the very difficult beauty of it. For the sonnet must not only deliver its burden of love, it must also deliver itself, and in so doing redeem for itself a magic that words (whether spoken, chanted, murmured, declaimed, hummed, intoned, or growled) will always have been relinquishing to song and dance.

Small wonder Wordsworth found even a 'brief' respite, ruminating the sonnet's scanty proportions. Its status in English poetry as one of the longest stanzas is one of courtesy, for the sonnet is a hybrid compounded of several measures. At least three stanzas contribute to its fixity of form and adaptability of rhyme scheme—the quatrain, the triplet or tercet, and the couplet. The quatrain is the 'workhorse' of English stanzas and gives the ballad its narrative stamina. It takes the initiative and the brunt of the burden in the sonnet too, comprising the first eight lines of the Petrarchan sonnet and the first dozen of the Shakespearean. The quatrain drags the load of the theme, frames the problem, and sets the scene and pace—it breaks into the silence of the page until the 'turn'. The triplet and tercet are more lightfooted than the quatrain, and they generally do the scouting and scooting which provides for the resolution after the turn. The difference between the triplet and the tercet is described by more than rhyme. The triplet piles up its effect by using one rhyme sound three times consecutively before advancing the cause of the next stanza with an entirely new triple rhyme sound. It promotes unity within each stanza, but does not enforce unity between stanzas. It seems suited, therefore, to the mood and pace of the exquisitely turned brief lyric. The tercet, on the other hand, trips along in *terza rima*. Its alternating rhyme scheme always has one foot in the door of the coming stanza with which it interlocks in rhyme and rhythm. It seems to effortlessly weave and unweave itself in preparation for what is coming. Like Penelope at her loom, the tercet undoes or loosens what it has completed in order to provide the excuse for continuing with a variation on the story. The tercet, therefore, is suited to the prophetic or adventurous long poem: it promotes a lively sublimation or delay of conclusion while it works the threads of the narrative. Exquisite enough in the haiku, the triplet or tercet finds a new orbit in the sestet of the sonnet, especially if it trips along with the spontaneity, fluency, and rapidity or *terza rima* or throws a playful light over the lucubrations deposited by the octave's sturdy quatrains. The sparkling triplet and cunning tercet, each in their own Latin way, bring about the desired release from the pressure that the more steady, Northern quatrains are made to contain.

Another stanzaic layer in the sonnet's laminated structure is the couplet. The couplet is not as volatile or versatile as the triplet or tercet, but it is witty, pointed, and climactic. In the Shakespearean sonnet the couplet provides not only the relief and resoluton but a miniature version, an epigrammatic playback, of the entire drama presented in the preceding three quatrains. Sometimes the couplet breaks the bubble of conflict with the pin of irony, sometimes it bravely puts an end to all bluffs and disguises, with an ace of hearts. In the Petrarchan sonnet the couplet can occur at various points: in the rhymed 'envelopes' of the octave (11. 2-3, 6-7), in the rhymed 'axis' (ll. 4-5) and anywhere in the sestet—in triple sequence, as complement to a quatrain, or as the axis of two tercets or triplets with inversely corresponding rhyme schemes. Whether it clinches an argument, offers terms of peace and love, or relaxes the troubled heart into silence by the spectacle of awe and spiritual osmosis, the couplet tends to make for a mock surrender, a thickening keen for change, a concentrated phase of transition described by the phrase, 'Reculer pour mieux sauter' (a crouch before a leap or retreat without defeat). Aside from nonce forms of stanzaic organization (which the five, six, seven, eight, or nine line stanza suggests for the irregularly rhymed sonnet) there are still the possibilities which blank verse suggest for an unrhymed sonnet, a concern which extends beyond the limits of this essay. The outlines of three stanzaic building blocks—quatrain, triplet or tercet, and couplet—are present in all regular forms. These stanzas are less obtrusive in those samples which direct their thematic currency evenly and masterfully throughout the whole of one hundred and forty syllables; in outstanding achievements of sonnetry, the presence of form, all form, is subliminal—supportive of intense artistic expression and imaginative experience at all points. The overwhelmingly exquisite sonnet has no corners, only a roundedoutness full of breathing holes. Rhyme, meter, and stanzaic organization, therefore, are less conspicuous in a lyric sonnet when a high degree of line integrity obtains, than in a witty sonnet when articulations of impassioned argument closely follow rhythmic units of stanzaically predictable length. The same elements of versification almost disappear in a dramatic sonnet when enjambment or syncopation stretches or knots the rhythm, which has effect of sprung rhythm: it attenuates the principle of mosaic return or 'closure'—dealing with one thing at a time between stanzaically pronounced intervals of rhetoric, rhyme, and syntax.

Like some mountainside hermitage snug near the mountain's narrow top, the sonnet offers a large perspective. Yet the sonnet is commodious in illusion only—it is not roomy inside. Its form invokes the principle of imbalance. Its shape of two unequal parts, octave and sestet, overlays three or more even stanzaic units. The structural appeal of two unequal parts fused over three or more symmetrically arranged parts has something to do with the appeal that the crooked straightness of a walking stick makes. Bipartite in shape, the sonnet shows a periodic inclination in syntax and rhythm. Sometimes in one breath it musically sustains smaller units of phrase and cadence whose stature it magnifies into more momentous perspectives by its 'turn' or emptied moment at the fulcrum of the eighth or ninth line. The numinous quality of the turn and the mediating propulsion of the periodic sentence in some of the greatest sonnets set all one hundred and forty syllables of its fourteen lines chiming in unison behind its burden like a crystal wine glass rubbed at the rim by a moist finger. Some of the more recalcitrant and philosphical sonneteers even resemble weight lifters as they move through the form—lift a weight up to the shoulders in one haul of the octave; pause a moment to borrow strength from somewhere in space and time at the turn; and make the jerk or elevation above the head in the sestet. In an attitude of rapt attention, the sonnet is both intuitive and analytic to an acute degree because it joins what it divides or finds divided. The turn represents a memory of the abyss—makes the figure a leap of faith makes—and reminds us symbolically of the strophic function of rhyme and meter in ancient Greek odes and Hebrew verse scriptures where it signals a change in direction to dancers and singers, a modulation in theme, mood, and attitude, to accommodate the wisdom of the oracle, chorus, or 'deus ex machina,' or to signal a change in tone from lyric or lamentative to prophetic or transcendent in the supplicant addressing his tribe, soul, and God. So strong is this bias to the turn in poetry close to its source of divine frenzy and controlled rage that even in the Shakespearean sonnet the Petrarchan turn occupies a residual status, like a pleat in cloth never completely removed by ironing, at about the eighth or ninth line, before it recurs emphatically in the penultimate line of the clinching couplet.

For all its brevity, the 'sonetto' ('small sound' or 'little song') compensates by its power of magnification and refraction. Wordsworth, for example, compares the sonnet, because of this magnifying power, to "an orbicular body, a sphere or a dewdrop." Its concentrated focus allows for a ubiquity of address that is difficult to match. And so the sonnet Dante first installed in the vernacular is all of one hundred and forty syllables the stiffest exercise in freedom the poet may choose to face. Its specifications are so exacting that since its eclosion nearly seven hundred years ago, masters of stichic, strophic, and stochastic forms have found themselves repudiating this most exotic of English stanzas. The Augustans—Pope, Swift, Dryden, for example—despite their aspiration to 'What oft was thought, but ne'er so well expressed,' (and possibly because of it) deliberately discarded the sonnet for their major poetic purposes. Some of the prime Romantics—Blake and Burns make a telling pair—for all their great love of vocal plasticity, overlooked the opportunity the sonnet provides for wit, melodic elan, and compression. The Romantics themselves were less concerned with conforming to the norms of society, or with satirizing false pretenses, than with visiting secret recesses of the soul, and salvaging sanctuaries of spirit and feeling invaded by the spread of industrialization; and Wordsworth and Keats used the sonnet form easily, often, and unselfconsciously. Some of Clare's sonnets, irregular in form, are now coming into circulation, and they reflect a direction—the jouncy rural still life and portrait reminiscent of Breughel's peasant scenes—which his contemporaries did not delve into but the experiments of the imagists now place in a new, and possibly more elevated, perspective. The Victorians, who relished musical pith in their elegant stanzas, to some degree mismanaged it for their decorative needs when they denuded the sonnet of the earthy, nomadic vitality Clare had restored to it. Some of the sonnets, not all, of Mrs. Browning and Dante Rossetti, even Poe, seem either overstuffed like pompous furniture in a deserted mansion, or full of bric-a-brac and cobwebs, when compared for vigour in diction and imagery to the sonnets of Renaissance masters like Donne. But since the same criticism holds for many of Wordsworth's sonnets (as Arnold would be the first to protest, and Arnold places him fifth in the ranks of poets) and since this criticism applies to the less spectacular samples by sonneteers of all times, Shakespeare included, perhaps the observation can be shunted away from the corners of the Victorian imagination to the bracing status of a generalization. As stated at the outset, the sonnet needs a periodic overhaul in subject, rhythm, imagery, rhyme, syntax, and diction before it can yield its ichor. Keats was keenly aware of this need, and his observations herald the misgivings of the twentieth century imagists.

On the Sonnet

If by dull rhymes our English must be chained,
    And, like Andromeda, the sonnet sweet
Fettered, in spite of pained loveliness;
Let us find out, if we must be constrained,
    Sandals more interwoven and complete
To fit the naked foot of poesy;
Let us inspect the lyre, and weigh the stress
Of every chord, and see what may be gained
    By ear industrious, and attention meet;
Misers of sound and syllable, no less
Than Midas of his coinage, let us be
    Jealous of dead leaves in the bay-wreath crown;
So, if we may not let the Muse be free,
    She will be bound with garlands of her own.

If Montaigne hung the motto 'Que scay-je?' (What do I know?) up in our imagination, Keats with his syncopated cadences and shaggy irregular rhymes has reminded every poet attempting the sonnet, to find 'Sandals more interwoven and complete/To fit the naked foot of poesy.' At these instigations, one Victorian went to work: Hopkins, whose powerfully innovative poetics have provided the basis and illustration for most serious experiments in poetry since, stimulated a few poets of the Atomic and Nuclear Age to apply some of their best energies to the form.

Given this periodicity—the sonnet has attracted few poets in any age except the Renaissance—it comes as a pleasant surprise to discover that many poets of all times have used the sonnet, even if only once, to create a successful occasional poem, what Rossetti called 'a moment's monument.' From Thomas Wyatt, who introduced the Italian prototype to Europe and first worked it into English form for generations after him to enjoy and use, to Robert Frost, who has given all variants of the sonnet a most unassuming but unmistakeable twist of his own, the list of poets who have utilized this fourteen liner is long and illustrious. Here is a sonnet census which includes in chronological order, poets from England, Ireland, Scotland, Wales, America, and Canada: d'Orleans, Wyatt, Surrey, Spenser, Raleigh, Sidney, Daniel, Drayton, Fletcher, Shakespeare, Donne, Herbert, Milton, Gray, Cowper, Wordsworth, White, Hunt, Byron, Shelley, Clare, Keats, Beddoes, Hood, Browning, Trench, Tennyson, Turner, Longfellow, Poe, Marston, Arnold, Meredith, Rossetti, Austin, Butler, Swinburne, Blunt, Symonds, Hardy, Lang, Bridges, Hopkins, Lee-Hamilton, Meynell, Gosse, Henley, Stephen, Wilde, Lampman, Dowson, Johnson, Douglas, Santayana, Yeats, Mew, Robinson, Belloc, Frost, Masefield, Babcock, Pound, Brooke, Jeffers, Ransom, Aiken, MacLeish, Owen, Welles, Millay, Cummings, Blunden, Tate, Adams, Winters, Campbell, Moore, Kunitz, Warner, Auden, Spender, Hassall, Gawsworth, Barker, Thomas, Berryman, Manifold, Lowell, Avison, Cogswell, Wright, Nemerov, Larkin, Acorn, Jennings, Hall, Hollander, Hill, Berrigan, Heaney, Solway, van Toorn, Gold, Norris, and McGee. The list could easily be extended by inclusion of more poets from the Nuclear era, but it would only gain in depth and variety if widened in linguistic range to contact poets who have worked, or are working, in French, Spanish, Italian, Portuguese, German, Yiddish, Hebrew, Polish, Russian, and the Scandinavian and Slavic languages.

Why poets have periodically resorted to the sonnet's fixed form to express some of their urgent concerns is difficult to answer unless the very philosophic notion of freedom in life and art is brought up. If 'Nature imitates art,' as Wilde insists, and nature seems nowhere so much without specifications of design and purpose that we are not still trying to uncover it, then it seems inconsistent to expect art to advance in expression without restrictions, free from references to a common language and form. Stravinsky maintains that "The more art is worked on, limited . . . the freer it becomes.' Eliot has said that 'No verse is free for the man who wants to do a good job.' And Frost has compared writing free verse to playing tennis without a net. The concern with fixed form, with the compression of rhythm into a stable artifact immune from the process of decay and phonetic fossilization, is perhaps only the obverse of our perennial fascination with chaos and the hold it has on us. Frost, who sometimes felt he was 'the only person going who works on any but a worn out theory . . . of versification,' confesses his fascination with chaos and the dark as a poetic motivation:

> My poems—I should suppose everybody's poems—are set to trip the reader head foremost into the boundless. Ever since infancy I have had the habit of leaving my blocks, carts, chairs, and such like ordinaries where people would be pretty sure to fall forward over them in the dark. Forward, you understand, *and* in the dark.

But he has also written that 'Nature within her inmost self divides/ To trouble men with having to take sides.' From this stoic's point of view, 'every poem is a momentary stay against the confusion of the world.' Frost does not lean on the comfort or truth of belief; his New England conservatism precludes Eliot's faith in the Logos, and possibly preempts it. His poetic conservatism blinds him, perhaps, to the jazzy and more mystic intuitions to be found in the poetry of Imagists such as Lawrence; he certainly appears jealous of the attentions Eliot receives for those innovations, especially those involving any social and religious vision of man, which he believes belong outside the poem. Perhaps his demon presses him too hard, for he has juxtaposed the need for form with the need for working in silence, as coeval with the cure for madness, poetic or other:

> Any psychiatrist will tell you that making a basket, or making a horseshoe, or giving anything form gives you a confidence in the universe . . . that it has form, see. When you talk about your troubles and go to somebody about them, you're just a fool. The best way to settle them is to make something that has form, because all you want to do is get a sense of form.

Frost's insistence here on form seems a little heartless. It is, after all, not form but feeling which counts. Frost's stubborn stress on form is less enlightened than Socrates' relation to his demon would endorse. Frost invokes the old Greek gods, but provokes the American (not New England) traits: rugged individualism, self-reliance, pragmatism, and chauvinism. But then Frost is complex and often proleptic: he has the good taste (as Baudelaire would chip in) to contradict himself now and then. In a lighter mood, he confesses that for him 'Poetry is like a cry,' even like a 'blush—you can get something you didn't know you had.' Perhaps, from this perspective, Frost's addiction to form is a kind of ritual sticktoitiveness, a belief in the human capacity for redemption through verbal meditation, through dramatic consummation. Frost's fear echoes not only Yeats' cry that 'The centre cannot hold' but our own Nuclear sensibility as well. To create a formless expression (if the term isn't tautological) seems to herald a giving way to, rather than a celebration of, the forces which beg to be instructed. The history of destructiveness is the history of our failure to imagine, and supply empathetic and imaginative forms to, the forces which threaten to destroy us. But the impulse to give imaginative heartfelt form is not the same as giving technical form. The threat of perpetual holocaust illustrates the differences between the two kinds of form amply and terrifyingly.

Another possible answer to the question, why poets of many cultures and times have made the pilgrimage to the sonnet's door (the image is revealing), lies in the direction of fashion, the appeal, perennial it seems, of exotic places and times, of mythic beginnings, of some Golden Dawn before the recorded history of a people. The invention of the sonnet is sometimes credited to the Sicilian poet Jacopo de Lentini, who lived, loved, and wrote in the first half of the thirteenth century. The sonnet, therefore, seems to have rustic roots. It appears at least half a century before it becomes immortalized by Cavalcanti, Dante, and Petrarch. This almost anonymous origin of the sonnet promises a certain lustre of naïveté and spontaneity. Borrowed from the Italians, a people with a much longer civilization than the European nations, and with a renown for technical ingenuity (ancient Rome being known for its bathrooms, aqueducts, and civil engineering as Canada is for the documentary), the sonnet may have secretly flattered the European nations which adopted it. The sonnet, after all, was not only the form Dante used to install the vernacular (spoken Italian) in, thereby giving dignity to the voice of the people at a time when classical learning was enjoying a rediscovery, but it was by its structural make up more republican than the feudal, and later, more democratic than the monarchic, systems of England, France, and Spain could officially ratify. The sonnet as a form, therefore, may have appealed to European poets by force of its illicitness: it gave Europeans a sneak preview of things to come. And then it also represented to an English and French court the zenith of courtly achievement overseas: the sonnet enshrined the new values of the Renaissance, perfection in literary and musical expression as well as in the chivalric devotion to courtly love. To write a sonnet was at one time, as the flood of both excellent and mediocre garlands of sonnets in vogue during the sixteenth century manifests, a conventional way of dissembling sophistication, of aspiring to an international jet set of poetic values. The sonnet was once in danger of Bovarization; it was the easy formula, replete with stock epithets, to which every 'miles gloriosus' and petty social climber could resort to appeal to the fantasy of his lady. Donne responded fiercely, circulating his poems in manuscript form among friends and connoisseurs. Shakespeare reacted savagely and deflated the pretensions of many sonneteers who applied the form without talent or conviction (in 'My mistress' eyes are nothing like the sun'). Perhaps Shakespeare's mockery of the standard list of comparisons used by mediocre sonneteers is less of a parody on extant practice than a sarcastic exhortation to sincerity in poetry and love. Perhaps. It is a question for imagists to ponder.

However we choose to answer the question (although there are reasons to believe the issue is no longer relevant: poets of the Nuclear age feel that the form is dead) we must, in speaking of the sonnet as a preterite form, come to its temperamental and technically elusive nature. It seems to require as much fine tuning as an Italian racing car, and as much dramatic sense of timing as a trapeze act. We might as well concur with Wyatt's unintentional description of the sonnet as it arrived fresh from the Continent:

> *Noli me tangere*, for Caesar's I am,
> And wild for to hold, though I seem tame.

The lines cited do suggest how difficult a lady to please Anne Boleyn was—her 'Don't touch me' challenge, if not characteristic of all English ladies of the court at the time, was probably more provocative than most poets of the time could withstand. Petrarch declares the same thing about his unearthly Laura. Wyatt's couplet at least confesses how intimidating the obstacles in the sonneteer's way are. In the same 'Whoso List to Hunt,' Wyatt states that the art of making a sonnet consists of emulating the wiles of the hunter and lover, of fashioning a 'net' with which to capture or 'hold the wind.' It must have been the sonnet's elusive and oracular nature, which Wyatt only hints at, that prompted Boileau to quip, or gasp in exasperation, a century later, 'In the sonnet the last line is all that counts.' Frost too has commented on the difficulty of having to 'cramp or stretch to come out even' in a total of fourteen lines. Perhaps this difficulty is only of an imagined erotic limitation, but Hopkins scaled some of his sonnets down to a ten and a half line

'Curtal' sonnet. 'When one goes so far,' he writes, 'as to run the rhymes of the octave into the sestet a downright prolapsus or hernia takes place and the sonnet is crippled for life.' It is well known that Welsh ladies were hard on Jesuit scholars, so Hopkins' chastening of the form breathes a kind of moonly fire. In the fourteenth century, Michelangelo, painting the ceiling of the Sistine Chapel from a cramped, supine position, wrote several sonnets in the spirit of burlesque and self-parody. The form he used is caudated: it is a regular sonnet with an added 'tail' of one or more rhymed tercets.

Regardless of the kind of sonnet in question, a signally reticent poise, hankered after density, imagist complexion, intricate vowel balance, strophic integrity, fluid periodic motion, and throaty syllabic charm are just a few of the features which have made the sonnet somewhat of a rare and celebrated beauty. Her taunt seems irresistible and calculated to deflate the resolutions of any but her most seasoned, persistent admirers. To Wyatt's inadvertent picture of the sonnet's inner workings, one is tempted to add Frost's meditation on its hidden springs, the creative forces of love, nature, and freedom as he describes them in his capriciously whispering Shakespearean sonnet, 'The Silken Tent.'

Besides presenting a venue to expressions of the amatory kind, from calls of courtesy and compliment, to catcalls and bursts of passion, the sonnet has also explored the primary religious emotion of awe and its aesthetic concomitant of surprise. Perhaps more than any other fixed forms except the still largely Oriental haiku, the western sonnet contains the canon of poetic utterances on the subjects of 'agape,' death, salvation, immortality, the feeling of going in and out of sync with the supernatural, and the poetically, if not philosophically, orthodox principle of pantheism. In one of his Holy sonnets, Donne apostrophizes

> At the round earth's imagined corners, blow
> Your trumpets, angels; and arise, arise
> From death, you numberless infinities
> Of souls, and to your scattered bodies go;

In another, he buttonholes Death himself with 'Death, thou shalt die,' registering accurately and passionately one of those critical moments of doubt and recovery taking us into the surd element of experience. Donne's rhetorical address takes into account not only the historical aspect of the times, when plague was often as fatal as cancer is in our century, but he addresses himself to an apocalyptic vision of man; he offers us imaginative release from slavery to temporal decay through the principle of revelation. Though several poets have dallied with the sonnet to celebrate the dimension of the sacred in the Nuclear age, poets coming into prominence since the forties have for the most part sought to incline their more socially urgent moral and imaginative concerns into stichic and stochastic forms. Nothing like the Holy sonnets of Donne or the Terrible Sonnets of intense devotion and nervous breakdown by Hopkins come to mind.

This rejection by most poets in the past four decades of not only the sonnet and fixed form, but of all poetry involving rhyme and meter, shows a return to a prosaic inclination. An age prone to stichic assimilation in verse betrays a predilection for reason over rhyme, statement over suggestion, definition over rune, and confession over apostrophe. The sonnet does not work well off an attitude given to secular norms and the paradigms of statistics. It requires the dimension of vision, the belief in the existence of a transcendent unity, and it urges a resolution of the conflict between sacred and profane. With the unswerving patience of Job, the sonnet stubbornly insists on a core of meaning that will adamantly defy the brunt of the most potent blast man or nature can deal out. It invokes the untroubled confluence of yin and yang, and steps gingerly on the dragon's tail, seeing in that oriental flying serpent the connubial alignment of male and female. In this sense, the sonnet is a butterfly skipping with impunity through the hot open mouth of a tiger caught for a moment by the mystery of the Tao.

At the root of the conception of poetry which the sonnet epitomizes in the West lies the art of song and dance. These rely on reiterative means, on rhyme-measured intervals, rhythmically dramatized pictures in sound, and patterns of expectation and fulfillment. Premised on this conception of harmony, the sonnet further stems from the notion of 'condensare,' 'dichtung,' or condensation. Poetry, whose units of sound, image, significance, and spiritual flow are aboriginally tiny, condenses as it slows down or accelerates into a time whose locus it shares with song and dance. This condensation of poetry with conviction in rhyme, in 'moving easy in harness' (as Frost phrases it), gives the word its elation and elasticity, its metaphoric power to magnify by suggestive denseness, its capacity for memorable ubiquity, for reverberating in the very consciousness it is an emblem of. This notion of 'accord' will have the poem compact and inevitable in design and purpose, like a seed. Rhyme in this scheme of things is not unfamiliar with the notion of rapid, disassociative juxtaposition, a feature a student once attributed to some of the poetry of Williams when she observed, 'Oh, his work is all bricks and no mortar.' But rhyme, at least in English, which lacks the natural musical fertility, the abundance of converging sounds that in some languages, Japanese or Italian, for example, soon make rhyme monotonous or redundant, resists the notion of fragmentation and discontinuity in favour of the maintenance of a metrical continuum. For rhyme discloses an organic point of view; it sees words organized in rows, with intimate contact, growing from the dramatic drive of the theme as 'leaves from a tree.' And if each leaf has its own unique shape, colour, and position in space, leaves share a collective identity. Rhyme in this scheme is much more complex and reciprocal than the repetition of words with nearly the same sound: it is a matter of intervals of letters, syllables, phonetic clusters, phrases, images, syntactic and rhythmic units with same or reversed sound, with implications of affinity and opposition, contraction and expansion, harmony and dissonance. Rhyme tries to invoke the very body and soul of language to stir the 'bones' of revelation. In a sonnet every consonant and vowel counts for rhyme, and for good reasons: not just to praise and propel all the atoms named by breathing from A to Z, but to breathe a numinous atmosphere (or the imitation of it in words) in and around the sense-carrying particles of sound, to provide the means of their elate propulsion, much as semen carries and propels the sperm that life swims in. Rhyme is half the meaning of a poem. Utility prose, whose function is blandly referential, abhors rhyme. The poet who relies on utility prose assumes rhyme to be some kind of starchy decoration or archaic organ, an unnecessary appendix for issuing obsolete matter into the void. The vertical friction of rhyme, and the rhythm it rides into, reinforced by diction, image, and metric organization, against the horizontal friction of syntax and idiom creates the dramatic tension that supplements the other half of a poem's meaning. That other half is theme, the particular stroke, which content offers, to make us 'hear, feel, and see.' The last phrase is Conrad's, and Conrad's prose is anything but utility prose. When he describes the traders steaming into 'The Heart of Darkness' firing at the natives and dismisses the spectacle with the phrase, 'squirting lead into the bushes,' he not only conjures up the folly and futility of men playing with war toys, but makes a corrosive attack upon the attempt at colonization: by reifying the image of onanism he prophecizes the sterility of the enterprise, and by subtly exploiting rhyme and rhythm, even in this brief phrase, he invokes the poisonous image of the nursery choking the infant and so plays the drums of doom to man's infantility.

In this sense of a dense liberated articulation, a sonnet is a giant haiku full of strange caesuras. And like the haiku, it shows refinement, vigour, and simplicity. It leaves no trace of effort. A good sonnet moves with casual subtlety, a relaxed vitality, out of the conviction in brevity and the surpassing power of song. So it remains an artifact with all the resources for squeezing the most out of a theme. So vital and passionate at a formal level as to have the sonneteer by the throat, the sonnet demands a subtle opening and closing of vowels, and a seamless meshing of consonants, these two constituting the 'soul and bones' of language (a Talmudic notion). The sonnet also demands a swift handling of image, spoken idiom and syntax—a fine tuning of pitch, pause, accent, and suspension or curtailment, depending on the cues for intonation provided by the dramatic voice. And the sonnet insists on the incorporation of all these elements into measures of rhyme and meter allowing for a fusion of accentual, syllabic, accentual-syllabic, and quantitative, prosodic systems.

So for about eighty syllables the sonnet has it: a rhythm as packed as the burden it possesses to drop, and a rhyme scheme tilted at intervals to match the burden of the theme, with a promise of a chiming off—a promise kept to after the turn when for sixty syllables or so the burden is so rhythmically chimed out or resolved that the theme ends off on a lingering in the consciousness. To keep to his promise of a musical opening and closing motion, a design of resolution that is at once as harmonically suspended as it is rhythmically percussive, the sonneteer must wander into Dedalian labyrinths of rhyme. If he's not for a sesquipedalian diction, he has millions of syllables and phrases to choose from, and he only settles for one hundred and forty after each and every one of them rhymes with, or takes into account the rhythms, rhymes, and rhyme-intervals of, each and every other. His proper number of rhymes, therefore, is not the two alternating in the octave and the possible two or three lacing the sestet, but a total of one hundred and forty reverberating to the conspicuous end rhymes of the Petrarchan template. The same applies, in varying degrees, to the Shakespearean, Miltonic, Spenserian, Curtal, Burlesque, and Caudated sonnet form. All this may be a way of reasserting the traditional view of rhyme or poetry, as riding the right words into the right places at the right times and with the right spaces between them. It presumes the poem capable of receiving the best feelings and words crowding in. Inachievable, it is the moon hanging in the poet's mind.

This decussated rhyme, this conformation of words counterpointing, this net of chiming the syllables make crossing over at different intervals and at minutely different angles of vocal, semantic, and imagist incidence, allows for the melody or dramatic tone to show up against a metric background. And it is this nuance in the grid which brings the sonnet close to the kind of total plasticity in vocal form which Cezanne expresses as the development of Impressionism into a form more inevitable and memorable than Imagism. It is what makes the sonnet so exacting and challenging for a contemporary poet whose vision in rhythm or picture in sound is further monitored by strictures of vernacular diction and idiomatic syntax. By riding his rhyme out in a steadied rhythm, which the friction of syntax and metre provide or anticipate at critical points, and by developing his theme and melody along logical and syntactical frames of stanza units, using one kind of rhythm to coincide with the braking of sense, another to syncopate or 'bend and stretch' it, he emphasizes the theme in its dramatic trajectory and semantic ligature. It is by riding his rhythm into an over rhyme that he depicts his thinking mastered out of feeling in singing words. This over rhyme, which is what can set all the syllables chiming in unison, is sometimes hidden before the sonnet's turn only to reveal itself more boldly as it rides the sestet out, as if to throw a new net of feeling and sense retroactively over the octave. The analogy from surfing may assist in exposition. The basic metric continuum or rhythmic pattern that the sonnet's rhymes reinforce represents the total and regular motion of the sea, the steady lap and jog of the waves. The sonnet's critical momentum, achieved by the time the turn occurs, coincides with the breaking of the boiling comber. The dramatic slide through the pattern of all the syllables, delineating the burden of the song delivering itself out of doubt, indicates the surfer as he rides the comber from sea to shore. Another way of putting it is saying that the over rhyme works like the jazz improvisation or 'ad lib' on an old tune, and on the continued progression of percussive harmony of the musicians who are implying the tune that the soloist is extemporizing on.

In the light of the preceding remarks, the achievement of an adaptation of the sonnet becomes tantamount to innovation. Though it is not within the scope of this essay to elaborate, it may briefly be ventured that Frost's 'Mowing,' which is an irregularly rhymed sonnet, is really a specimen whose architectonics (with antecedents in Shelley's 'Ozymandias' and Keats' 'On the Sonnet') are so madrigalistic as to constitute a new development of this old fixed form that it anticipates experiments with free form and seriously calls for a review of the contemporary disdain for form. Though Frost with characteristic elfishness might repudiate it, as he repudiated all behaviourist descriptions of himself—he prided himself on his 'uncatchability' and claimed he was neither an extrovert nor an introvert but 'just a plain vert from Vermont'—a new type should be added to the list of forms: the Vermont or Frost sonnet. North of the border this has already been done.